Knee Deep

Dying to Lead

Dr. Shawn D. Foster

Knee Deep: Dying to Lead

Copyright © 2025 Dr. Shawn D. Foster

All rights reserved. No portion of this book may be reproduced in any form without permission from the author or publisher except as permitted by US copyright law.

This is a work of nonfiction; however, names, locations, personalities, and stories have been embellished or truncated to protect identities and convey the incidents' essence.

For permissions, contact ShawnFoster696@yahoo.com

ISBN: 9798280298507

Unless otherwise noted, Scripture quotations are taken from the ESV® Bible (The Holy Bible, English Standard Version®). Copyright © 2001 by Crossway, a publishing ministry of Good News Publishers. Used by permission. All rights reserved.

Scriptures marked NIV are from the Holy Bible, New International Version®, NIV®. Copyright © 1973, 1978, 1984, 2011 by Biblica, Inc.® Used by permission of Zondervan. All rights reserved worldwide. www.zondervan.com. The "NIV" and "New International Version" are trademarks registered in the United States Patent and Trademark Office by Biblica, Inc.®

Scriptures marked KJV are from the King James Version. Public domain.

Knee Deep

Contents

Introduction *1*
Part One: The Journey *5*
Dying *7*
Born to Lead *15*
Trained to Lead *21*
Quitting Time *26*
Winning Time *33*
Showing Up *40*
Staying Time *48*
Finding a Way *51*
Service Is the Journey; Leadership Is the Goal *56*
Showing Up 2.0 .... *62*
Showing Up 3.0 .... *66*
Losing Time *71*
Losing Time 2.0 .... *75*
Pole Position *78*
Bet on Yourself *84*
Taken *88*
Teachable Moments *92*
Part Two: The Two-Way Mirror *96*
Teachable Moments 2.0 .... *97*
Cancer *100*
Call My Bluff *103*
Beside Myself *106*
Death *112*
Ring the Bell *116*
Bridging the Gap *119*
Bridging the Gap 2.0 .... *126*
Bridging the Gap 3.0 .... *131*
Assignment *134*
Assigning Blame *139*
Assigned *148*
The Good Race *154*
Followers *159*
Faith *172*

About the Author 175
Acknowledgments 178
Quick Tips, Quips & Trips.. 181
Notes 184

Introduction

Are leaders born or made?
If leaders are *only* born, stop reading immediately. Ask for a refund. Burn this book. You cannot sharpen a sponge, so quit trying. Why read a book about becoming a better leader if leadership is only inherent? Let's solve this mystery.

I suppose we cannot solve the mystery if we cannot make leaders—or make leaders better. Some problems are unsolvable, after all. What's the perfect way to say, "Honey, I've been diagnosed with stage IV cancer"? We don't have one. Trust me, I've been there, and I know. We can, however, develop a leader's discernment to its highest capacity. And we can develop leaders. Let's solve this problem together.

Since you're reading this book, you've likely read the maxim *Leadership begins with self-leadership*—or something similar. If we can't lead ourselves, why should anyone follow? That's a great question born from a worn-out idea. That idea is well-worn because we overuse it. We bludgeon it to death. We have to. But why?

Those in leadership positions lead others *before* leading themselves. *We* attempt to lead others before we *can* lead ourselves. We want power, control, acknowledgment, and, dare I say it, legacy, before we've earned our keep, much less our stripes. We want to be crowned the "hero," behaving as if everyone needs to be rescued. We want the trophy before running a good race. This leads to my first point, and it's *not* about self-leadership. It's about communication.

I don't answer my rhetorical questions, which push individuals to think. The leader who asks rhetorical questions should not answer them. That's the audience's job. We must allow productive struggle; our audience needs to self-reflect and develop their methodologies. When I wrote, "If we can't lead ourselves, why should anyone follow?" I didn't answer the question. It's meant for you. I ask, you answer, and you keep all the benefits. That statement illustrates the first step in my 3-Step Communication Process.

GOOD LEADERS PROVIDE TOP-NOTCH COMMUNICATION.

3-Step Communication Process

1. Tell people what you're going to do.
2. Update them on the progress.
3. Tell them when you're done.

In this memoir, I will recount my leadership journey and provide anecdotal and experiential evidence to guide your journey. You'll read of tragedy, heartache, and loss as well as triumph, perseverance, and hope. I invite you to follow me through it. I'll maintain optimism. I'll use parables, aphorisms, maxims, epigrams, and proverbs to stimulate thought. I might even provoke a discussion or two.

Many want bulletproof, empirically-based answers to all their questions, and some may even label parables as trite. Well, we can want in one hand and . . . Since I'm writing to inform, engage, and stimulate, not to give people what they want, I utilize sayings that compel us to seek understanding (e.g., *I believe showing up without an answer beats staying home with one*). Leaders seek answers. If there's an unsolvable riddle, leaders teach good decision-making skills in the pursuit, and we update on progress while solving what we can.

To apply my second step, I'll update our progress throughout our time together.

Progress Update

I've listed my 3-Step Communication Process but haven't answered my rhetorical question, and we're not done yet.

I provide progress reports for two reasons: Progress reports keep people informed and validate completed work. Information increases understanding. Updates keep us accountable. What keeps you accountable?

Progressing through this leadership training requires accountability and responsibility. If you don't identify your intended growth, measure it, and responsibly communicate it to someone, you're just reading another book—and missing the magic. My memoir would just be entertainment in your hands or good vibrations in your ears rather than transactions in your heart. Do you want growth or just another book on an innocuous list?

Accountability and responsibility are not magic but fertilizer. And we all need fertilizer. So, I'll ask again: What keeps you accountable? I won't answer for you because I believe in *you*. You can identify a growth area, read the challenges, and find accountability. But then again, since I've mentioned you four times in this paragraph, who am I?

SHOWING UP WITHOUT AN ANSWER BEATS SKIPPING OUT WITH ONE.

I'm Shawn Foster, a student, teacher, husband, father, and leader. What gives me the right to write about leadership? Well, I've been in leadership development for over thirty years, and there's a difference between having thirty years of experience and having the same experience thirty times. Leadership is not repeating the same action for years. That's repetition. Leadership is repeating an action that others follow. That's influence.

Many times, the obstacles we lead others through are new obstacles, and good leaders prove that they can overcome obstacles like poverty, money, failure, success, fatherlessness, power, cancer, and spouses who tell us we've never been in their wildest dreams—maybe that's just mine. I've overcome many obstacles.

I have four advanced degrees, but they didn't prepare me to be the first African American deputy superintendent in one of the reddest counties in rural South Carolina. And yes, that also means the county board of education hired me. So, we both did something rare: They hired their first African American in that position, and I served in it. I had become accustomed to rarity; I kicked field goals in college.

I didn't see too many other placekickers on college football teams who looked like me, so I scored a spot as a wide receiver and team captain as well. Yet, none of those experiences prepared me to lead through a school shooting, let alone a second one. But the aggregate experiences played a part.

I grew up without money, but then I got some. I grew up uneducated, but then I got one. I gained some friends along the way, but then I lost some. I grew up without a father, but then I became one. I lived a good life, but when cancer came, I lost one.

We're nearly done with the introduction. The third step is telling you when we're done. We're done when we're dead. I'm serious. We're done leading when we die; ironically, we begin leading when we die because that leads to new life. It's a paradox. A wise man once said, "You must die to yourself daily." He also said, "You must be born again." There's wisdom to seek in that juxtaposition. Are you up for the task? Think I'll answer that for you?

Back to the opening question, "Are leaders born or made?" That's not rhetorical. It's a good question. I'll say *both* and *neither*. You'll need to follow me to see why. We're done with the introduction now, but we've only begun the journey. And we begin at the end: I learned leadership the day I died with cancer.

Part One: The Journey

Shawn Foster

Dying

I died with cancer. I didn't die of it. I didn't want to die. I had too much to lose: a beautiful wife, two endearing children, and a life-giving career. If you skipped the introduction, I'm sorry you missed it. That was my end. This is my life.

There's something to knowing a man in his dying hours, a clarity we gain in suffering. Questions arise. Did his mind darken while he looked with calloused eyes on the world? Did he pour out his soul in a deathbed confessional? Did he remain faithful to his purpose? Did he even know his purpose? Did he cry while he clung to his wife's hand, staring into the eyes of his children? Did he have miles of questions but only milliseconds to answer? Did he . . .?

In June 2018, my wife, Tanya, greeted me with a complaint.

"Shawn, your allergies are getting worse. I can't sleep; you're snoring is reckless."

"Well, good morning to you, too."

"I see you're smiling. You think this is funny?"

"Sweetie, people who work hard snore. So, if you want more sleep, I suggest you go to bed before me."

That was that . . .

I breezed through boatloads of paperwork that morning. For superintendents, the only summer break is the one we try to avoid due to the breakneck speed of summertime change. We open new schools, hire new staff, update facilities, attend myriad meetings, and fall just short of breaking our necks before convocation in August. I had just signed the final document weighing down my desk and immediately sent an email memorandum when I felt my phone vibrate.

Shawn Foster

"Hello, sweetie."
"Shawn, I made you an appointment with an ENT today."
"ENT? What are you talking about?"
"An ear, nose, and throat doctor for your snoring."
"Okay."
I'll tell her I'm too busy.
"I made it on your lunch break, so you can't say you're too busy."
"You know I don't always take lunch at the same time of day."
"I checked your calendar."
I'll just say I went. That'll keep her off my—
"You know I'm going to call them, right?"
"Huh? Call whom?"
"The doctor's office—to make sure you went."
"Okay, I'll go. What's the name of this place?"
That was that . . . Tanya had me in checkmate.

Tanya and I matched wits all the time, our little way of keeping things interesting. After fifteen years of marriage, we hadn't lost our spice. She pigeon-holed me that morning, but I'd get her back. I always did. She had it coming. Especially for this—valuing her sleep over my health—making me miss my lunch. We'd see how much sleep she would get.

The warm doctor's office didn't have the stale feeling I associated with medical facilities. I hadn't spent much time in any, but I'd visited others while they suffered. Much can be learned while sitting with the suffering: about them and about you. *How do you sit with those who suffer?*

I tapped my foot on the waiting room floor and checked my watch in the examination room chair when Dr. McMiniman finally did the courtesy knock and peeked inside.

"How are we doing?"
"Doc, if I were any better, I'd be two people."
"Since there's two of you, do you mind paying twice?"
"There might be two of me, but I'm not getting two checks!"
"But you can still help me move this couch, right?"
"Sure thing, give me a clean bill of health, and I'll send my wife right over."

"Then who'll be the second person?"

"Tanya and her mouth count for two."

"Sounds like you love her."

"I'd be dead without her, but for right now, I just want her to leave me alone."

"You don't want that. She might leave you *too* alone."

"Amen to that."

"What brings you in?"

"My wife says I'm snoring. I told her that hard workers snore, but she's not buying it. She's seen me do the dishes."

"Is she wrong?"

"Tanya's never wrong. Don't tell her I said that."

"Let's check your symptoms. Maybe we can help your Dallas Cowboys get a winning season while we're at it."

"Too soon, Doc. Too soon."

It had been five months since the Cowboys had last touched the field. While the doctor's cold fingers felt my glands and he inspected my nostrils with his light, I wondered how he knew I was a Cowboys fan. *Maybe he's telepathic . . .* What he said next nearly stopped my heart. At that moment, we were the only two individuals on earth with the knowledge that would change my life.

"I believe you have cancer."

I carefully inspected his eyes. "Doc, that ain't nothing to play about."

"I've done this for twenty-nine years. Let's hope I'm wrong for the first time."

Some Storms We Can't Predict

I often say, "We're tough on process and easy on people." We're too late if the storm hits before we make an emergency plan. My staff and I spend countless hours preparing for crises *before* they hit. We don't wait until they hit. When a crisis strikes, we don't wait, and we follow the process. If there's a breakdown, we don't waste it; we learn from it. We investigate the process and encourage the people. Nobody hurts when

Shawn Foster

we terminate a defunct process, but everyone hurts when we terminate a person's employment.

Quick Tips

> - Be tough on process and easy on people.
> - Prepare for the storm.
> - Never waste a good crisis.

But how do you tell your family a tornado ripped through the doctor's office, and you never saw it coming because those four walls don't have windows?

What do I tell my wife? I didn't check my watch. *What do I tell my kids?* I imagined their tears. *What about my mom and my grandma?* I sat up straight. *The school district?* I closed my eyes. *What if I die?* I took a deep breath.

He gave me his personal cell phone number and encouraged Tanya and me to call him if we had any questions before my next visit. We called him that evening. He gave us grim details about challenges we could potentially encounter. Three days later, we returned and got the CT scan results.

"Shawn, not only was I right that you have cancer, but it's stage IV nasopharynx squamous cell carcinoma."

We let that settle. Tanya looked at me. Stage IV. We hadn't told the kids.

"Doc, I have a question. I had lab work done two weeks ago, and my results came back clean. If this cancer didn't show in my bloodwork, how do other people find out?"

"They find out the same way you did, but most find out too late."

I also let that settle. *Okay, so it's stage IV. Can't go back now. Search for a solution.*

"What's the plan of action? What do we need to do?" The doctor gave me some advice that changed my life, became my rebirth.

"Shawn, this will be the toughest battle of your life. You will spend six to eight hours a day, five days a week, in the cancer center undergoing chemotherapy and radiation. We will administer chemotherapy, and then we'll hydrate you back to health. We'll poison you and then try to bring you back to life. *I need you to understand this:* There will be days you won't be able to get out of bed, days you can't walk, days you can't keep food down, days you'll be brought to your *knees*. What you do next is most important. If you stand a chance to beat this cancer, you have to do one thing. On the days you want to quit, *you must show up*. You have to show up."

You Must Show Up

I thought about walking into the hornet's nest—the unpopular place where people manufacture lies so I second-guess myself. I recalled decisions I'd made that hurt me personally but were right for the cause. I remembered being stuck—not knowing the right thing to do but making a decision and working through the outcomes. Doc was right. When the stakes were high and the chips were down, the worst I could do was not show up. That's abandonment. I must show up.

I never saw that storm coming, but I agreed to follow the process. "Okay, Doc. I'll show up."

Show Up, Show Up, Show Up

Tanya and I sat with red-rimmed eyes, developing a plan to tell the kids. We agreed on how we'd handle it. I'd do the talking. However, at the moment of truth, I deviated. I changed my story to benefit my children and my faith. Initially, Tanya got upset, but after I explained myself, she understood. That was the guy she hoped would show all along.

Progress Update

I'll give more details later about telling my wife and kids I had cancer. But for now, I'll tell you this: *Telling a hard truth is easier than covering up a soft lie.* Liars are soft.

Shawn Foster

While discussing details with close friends, mentors, and colleagues, I attended treatment throughout the summer. Doc wasn't wrong. Treatment stripped my life away and brought me to my knees. My health failed. I couldn't show up for work, but I showed up for treatment. I couldn't show up for dinner, but I showed up for treatment. I couldn't show up for practice, but I showed up for treatment. I showed up! Until I couldn't. I gave up on treatment.

On August 22, 2018, I quit. I couldn't do it. Dangling bedside, puking my guts out, I gave up. "I can't do this anymore." Tears dripped from my chin into the trash can. "I'm not going in today." I wiped my mouth. "I'm quitting treatment." Tanya calmly moved to my side.

We were already running late for the morning's appointment, and the traumatic tension broke me. I could barely breathe; I'd lost over fifty pounds and wasn't winning the battle. I was losing. So, I quit.

My phone buzzed on the nightstand. I threw up. It buzzed again. I wiped my mouth. My phone buzzed again. I caught my breath. It vibrated out of control while I clutched the sheets. Finally, I grabbed it, ready to heave it against the wall.

"Dr. Foster, you're such an inspiration to me." Tears welled in my eyes, not from gratitude but from the acrid fire in my throat.

"Dr. Foster, I know I can trust you. I respect you, man!" I sat up, taking short breaths.

"Dr. Foster, remember when you hired me—" I put the phone down. I couldn't read the messages. My body's automatic panic response took control. I threw up again, nearly falling. The phone vibrated desperately close to the edge. I pushed it away from the trash can. My stomach lurched. The phone buzzed. Again. And again. And again.

During convocation, my friend and the superintendent of schools, Dr. Sean Alford, requested well wishes and prayers for me. When 2,800 people pray for you, power seeps into your bones. *I could.* I got up and went to treatment.

Dr. Alford understood something every good leader understands: *All leaders need something to help them get up when they want to give up.* He helped me get up. I kept getting up, and I kept showing up. Until I couldn't.

Knee Deep

Live Your Obituary for Tomorrow You May Die

I have a challenge for you, and I pray you take it. All my administrators complete this assignment: We write our obituary and live by it. It's an unwritten requirement for employment—the kind of unwritten rule that changes lives, not because we follow the rule but because we embody the spirit. Everyone wholeheartedly agrees to the assignment when I sit cross-legged in my office, explaining it over smiles and coffee. However, when they face the task, they beg me to rename the assignment to give it a more updated, vision-casting tone. Death unnerves them. I respond, "I would rename it if death weren't required."

It's your obituary. What do you want written after you're gone? When you can't defend yourself to yourself or others, how will your life read? I don't answer those questions for them, and I refuse to help them. It's theirs. And I believe letting them squirm communicates my belief in them. I have confidence they'll finish. Everyone does, and nobody's died from it yet.

I wrote mine long before my cancer; my cancer just punctuated it, made it real. In my obituary, I wrote soul-stirring attributes like "compassionate, faithful, dedicated, confident, and leader." Descriptions that stirred *my* soul. I included inspirational quotes, such as, "Let us say, God put me among these scenes, these people, these opportunities, these duties. He is neither absent-minded nor incompetent. This is exactly the place He means me to be in, the place I am capable of filling: there is no mistake. My life is in its proper setting."[1] I included my favorite scripture about the wise man who built his house upon the rock and found himself safe in the storm.[2] I attributed any success to my family and faithful friends and requested that those who knew me invest their lives in the next generation. I've done mine; you do yours.

Who Rings the Death Knell?

Even with prayer chains praying and friends manifesting health and wellness, my health fell apart. I was glad I'd written my obituary before my illness. In my trial, I knew my direction, and I'd accepted my challenge and faced it with fury. I showed up, but the sun rose on a day *I* couldn't do it anymore. On September 10, 2018, I gathered Tanya, my two children, Alyx and Aden, and gave my deathbed confession.

We gathered in the living room, the same place where I had told them I'd be all right, and I saw tears leaking from their big, brown eyes. I felt my heart beat against my chemo port, my feeding nub ached in my abdomen, and my esophagus flaked into ash. What did I have left? A skeleton of a man, sixty-five pounds lighter than when I started, I looked at them through hollow eyes.

"I DON'T THINK YOUR DAD'S GOING TO BEAT THIS CANCER THING."

Aden squinted, and Alyx covered her mouth. A fourth grader and a seventh grader, both facing their father's impending death, both witnessing weakness from a dad who didn't dare speak of defeat. "I'm okay not beating this cancer thing; it's in God's hands now." The tears fell from their little faces. "But I need you to do something for me when I'm gone . . ."

I did something no dad ever wants to do but something every father should get the opportunity to do. I told them I'd be leaving, but I also told them how much I loved them before I'd gone. *Good leaders provide top-notch communication.*

Everything felt final. I was in over my head. That night, through salty tears and spilled guts, I spoke to my wife and mom. I told them the family would be okay. I'd fought the good fight and finished the race. I felt at peace. I was okay going under.

In my bedroom alone, before Tanya joined me, I hit my knees. "I'm done; I'm through fighting." I got knee-deep that night, and then I pulled myself into bed, rolled over, and puddled the pillow. I didn't cry for me; I cried for them. Who would help them when I was gone? I decided again it was in God's hands, and if he needed me, he would keep me around.

He let me die.

Born to Lead

"Get up. Get up, son; it's time to get up. You've got to walk through the house, usher in the new year, bring us luck. Shawn, you hear me? It's time to get up."

I rubbed my sleepy eyes awake, pulled the bedcovers away, and rolled onto the cold floor. My pajama shirt cinched near my naval, too small, last year's model. At Mom's bed, I rested, yawning myself awake. *What time is it? What do I do again?* I couldn't remember, so I climbed into her bed and fell asleep.

"Shawn, we need you awake, baby. Got to get up. Now get through there."

"What do I do again, Momma?"

"You walk through the house. You are the man of the house here. When you walk through the house first, it brings good luck."

"Where do I go?"

I rubbed my eyes again, trying to comprehend, ready to do anything to get back in bed.

"To the door and back. All you need to do is walk through the house, just like we talked about earlier."

"Then I can go back to bed?"

"Then you can go—"

I'm not sure I heard another word. I scooted through the rooms barefooted, sleepwalking in the new year. I squeezed past boxes, between tables and chairs, under hanging clothing, touched the door, and scurried back to the bedroom. When the coast was clear, everyone cheered. I got tons of hugs and kisses, and I fell back into bed, a leader.

Understated, my family was superstitious. Euphemistically, they embodied their culture. Realistically, it was all a little bit crazy, but that

Shawn Foster

New Year's Eve trek through our three-bedroom apartment galvanized my first understanding of leadership: *The best leadership decisions often come from those who commit to following the leader.*

Surrounded by strong women, I saw leadership take many roles. My grandma, Martha, led the home: her rules, her way. She didn't rule with an iron fist but with encouragement, always believing we could better ourselves. We lived in a cramped apartment with her, sharing it with Mom's siblings: Monica, Terri, Cheryl (Mom's twin sister), Regina, and Lynn, along with two cousins, Keisha and Tameka. Yes, my grandma, six daughters, two granddaughters, and me. Ten total. Then she brought in April—a little girl who lived in the same projects—which made eleven.

Outnumbered ten to one, you can imagine that I saw leadership take many different roles but that I didn't do much leading. I followed. I had to, by design. Authority is bestowed by authority. That's a fancy way of saying we can't truly earn authority; it must be given to us. I had no authority. I barely had pajamas. When instructed to take out the trash, I took it out. When informed it was bedtime, I went to bed. When told to sweep the kitchen, I swept the kitchen. I didn't lead, but they gave me ample opportunities to follow.

On New Year's Eve, they told me to walk through the house, and I obeyed. Following their instructions allowed me to contribute—something I cherished. I led in the new year, but I did it by permission. Over time, I held on to that feeling, that position. They honored me as the man of the house, although I had only recently learned to put down the toilet seat. Sure, they followed a gender-biased tradition, but by following, they influenced me to desire that responsibility, to become dependable for others. They shaped my mindset.

Quick Tips

> - Deciding to follow the leader is a leadership decision.
> - Authority is bestowed, not taken.
> - We must give people a taste of leadership to see if they're hungry.

Knee Deep

"Shawn, it's time to—dang, son! Have you been in here waiting?"
"Yes, ma'am."
"Then why didn't you come out?"
"I wanted to be ready when you called for me, but you didn't call."
"I'm calling you now. It's time."

Mom and I eventually moved to a project apartment in Greensboro, North Carolina, and while the world grew up around us, and I grew up as the single child of Sheron Foster, the time came when I no longer had to be called. I showed up because I wanted to. But before my little heart could understand and my mind could conjure that "God doesn't always send the equipped; he equips whomever he sends," I learned to want to be called, even in my too-tight pajamas.

After Mom and I moved, I gained more authority. I rang the bell for the city bus. Actually, they needed me to ring it because if I didn't, how would passengers know their next stop? I had a job to do, and I took it very seriously. Eight-year-olds do that. They commit responsibilities to heart.

I woke up early. Mom had the oven open and a pot of water heating on the stove. She plugged the kitchen sink and filled it. As the steam rose and I inhaled that warm air, I tested the water with my hands. Just right. I washed up and returned to the bedroom to dress. The city bus driver Mr. Greg needed me.

After breakfast, Mom closed the oven, and we cleaned the kitchen. Back then, I didn't know about separate electric and gas bills or the austere measures that mothers take to divide between the two to protect the children they love. I knew I had hot water in a kitchen sink and a warm place to eat breakfast. I knew we saved our coins and measured our distances in bus fare cents.

From our apartment, we walked briskly through the cold, hand in hand sometimes, and made it to the bus stop early. Mom bit her top lip and tied a shoestring around my neck with an emblem of love hanging to my chest. That house key meant I'd have a way to get in while she finished her day at work. She pulled me close by my jean pocket and stuffed thirty-five cents into my coin pocket, then made me promise to protect it.

"I promise, Momma. I'm always careful with my money."

Shawn Foster

"I know, but if you lose it, who will bring you home to me?"

"Momma, Mr. Greg would bring me home; he'd never leave me behind."

"Let's protect that money, just in case."

As I walked to the bus, something lingered in Mom's stare. She had emotions I couldn't understand at the time, like something uncontrollable could happen to her little Black son on the way to school. I couldn't name the emotion; I could only sense it.

I climbed the bus steps and waved goodbye as Mr. Greg called, "Good morning, Shawn Foster!"

"Good morning, Mr. Greg."

The bus passengers cheered when I boarded the bus; without me, who would pull the bell? I took my rightful seat, and at every stop, Mr. Greg gave me the nod, and I'd ring the bell. At the next stop, I'd do the same. All the way down the line until we reached the school bus stop. There, Mr. Willie was waiting.

Mr. Willie didn't have a bell on his bus, so I relaxed on my second ride. However, just like Mr. Greg, Mr. Willie always greeted me kindly and treated me with respect. Some kids didn't treat him with respect, but Mr. Willie had character; he didn't allow their actions to disrupt his. And he didn't allow others' expectations to trump his expectations for himself.

I discovered this one morning when the city bus ran late. Mom waited with me at the bus stop, and we waited, waited, waited, but Mr. Greg didn't show. We turned to walk home, Mom mumbling something beneath her breath about figuring out what to do, when I heard the familiar sound of the bus hydraulics. I turned and saw Mr. Greg driving to the stop. I began to run.

"Shawn!"

"Yes, Momma!"

"Check your coins. You got them?"

"Right here."

"Key?"

"Still tied."

"Have a good day at school. I love you."

"I love you too!"

Knee Deep

And I booked it to Mr. Greg, who had a frazzled but cheerful look on his face.

"I'm sure glad you're here, buddy. I thought you might be gone, and we'd have nobody to ring the bell."

Although they were late, the passengers cheered for me when I boarded. I had no understanding of the concerns that adults set aside to adulate the future generation, just that I needed to ring the bell. Mr. Greg drove hurriedly. "Shawn, we have to move quickly. I don't want you to miss Mr. Willie."

"Okay. I'll be fast."

Everybody seemed worried that everybody else would leave me, but I had no worries. And rightfully so. When we rounded the corner, Mr. Willie's yellow school bus sat just as I expected, the double doors open, waiting for me. I rang the bell, jumped from the city bus, and raced to the school bus, Mr. Greg honking all the while.

I called out, "Good morning, Mr. Willie! They were so afraid you'd leave me, but I said you'd never leave me."

"You're right, son. I'd never leave you."

Quick Tips

> - Leaders look for other leaders to help when they can't.
> - Character doesn't allow others' actions to disrupt it.
> - Leaders finish before they leave.

Mr. Willie proved himself trustworthy. That wasn't the only time the city bus ran late, and the school bus ran late plenty of times, too. But nobody left me.

I didn't have a male figure at home, but I had those two men who drove buses and gave me respect, whether it was warranted or not. That's not to say I didn't have male leadership in my life, and that's not to discount the female leadership I had. Instead, I'm highlighting the leadership two men taught me though they had nothing to gain from it.

So, who led whom? Did my grandma and aunts lead when they followed the tradition and had me walk the house on New Year's Eve? Did my mom lead, entrusting me to God with that burning fear in her

Shawn Foster

eyes, tying a key to my neck? Did Mr. Greg lead, allowing me to ring the bell, giving me something to be proud of? Did the bus passengers lead by cheering when a little boy made the bus in time? Did Mr. Willie lead by never leaving me behind, even though he had all those other kids to get to school? Did I lead by showing up? Do you?

> THE BEST LEADERSHIP DECISIONS OFTEN COME FROM
> THOSE WHO COMMIT TO FOLLOWING THE LEADER.

Trained to Lead

I have an agenda. I'm both telling a story and teaching a lesson. I understand some folks understand better when extracting principles from a story, while others grow deeper when analyzing the facts of a statement. Fiction versus non-fiction. Some choose poetry, others choose prose. Aesthetes prefer drama; scientists desire data. The educator in me empathizes with both, while the leader in me sympathizes with neither. Maybe there's a dichotomy. Maybe this is my digression: Context matters.

My agenda requires I give you both options to better facilitate understanding; however, my intuition tells me it doesn't matter how much I give: *What matters is how much you get.* Plainly, I want you to develop the skill of discernment. I want you to choose *when.*

Discernment requires more, and that's why we shy away from it. It's easier to quote Shakespeare or memorize a formula than to use discernment. Pointing back to a rule gives us a sense of control, but leaning into discernment creates peace. We know 2 + 2 = 4, and we can tell a noun from a verb, but when do we give each person two, and when do we give all four to one? When do we say, "Love never fails," and when do we love failures?

Following is a list of statements. Some are aphorisms, some are admonitions, some are logical, and some are statistics.

- You should not give a magnifying glass to worry.
- We're tough on process and easy on people.
- You must show up.
- Sometimes you're first; sometimes you're the secret sauce.
- Leaders don't have all the answers; they just know to seek.

- An organization led by one ceases to be an organization.
- The battle is yours; the success is shared.
- The battle is yours; the results are not.
- He is no fool who gives up what he cannot keep to gain what he cannot lose.[3]
- Good leaders don't give up 50 percent of $1 million to get 100 percent of $10.
- Only 40 percent of leaders report their organizations have high-quality leadership.[4]

Each of those statements can be misapplied. A leader could implement the admonition, "You must show up," and fail to apply discernment, leading to demise. In fact, one did: Julius Caesar.

From his assassination, we gained the idiom "stabbed in the back." History records that conspirators persuaded him to show up at the Senate, then stabbed him. Talk about a double-edged dagger. The man denied being crowned king in a show of servility, only to be killed for declaring himself "dictator for life" in a show of loyalty. He showed up despite multiple warnings not to go. His wife, friend, and even a fortune teller warned him, but he showed up anyway. Plutarch's *Lives* indicates Caesar showed up from a sense of duty, while Shakespeare's *Julius Caesar* emphasizes Caesar's hubris.

While we don't know why Caesar showed up, we know he lacked discernment *when* he did. So did the conspirators. His assassination led to a great civil war, and many of them died because of it. Their coup crippled the economy, the people, and themselves. What do you think? Should everyone have just stayed home?

Caesar should have. However, if a leader fails to show up for the people, such as Ashraf Ghani when he fled Afghanistan in 2021, they would be labeled as cowardly. Caesar "showed up," and it led to his demise. Ghani fled, proving his cowardice. Do I show, or do I go? In *Knee Deep,* we'll find an answer.

Let's review a statistic: "Only 40 percent of leaders report that their organizations have high-quality leadership." At face value, that suggests that people don't trust their leadership, but look closely: *Leaders* report . . . ! Talk about circular reasoning. Does this mean leaders don't trust their leadership? One could read this and believe that trust in leadership has eroded—or *have* their trust in leadership eroded.

How do we know when to believe what and what to believe when?

That's not a rhetorical question. It's an actionable one, and it supports my agenda. I want leaders to become *discerning* leaders. We can develop discernment; it's a gift and a skill. Just like running fast or singing soprano, discernment can be learned, but the degree to which it can be learned is limited.

When people ask, "Does effort create ability?" I say, "Yes, if capacity is unlimited." That's a kind way of saying no. Capacity matters but is always limited for humans. If you fill a gallon jug to the top, you can't fill it any further, no matter how much water you add. Effort enhances ability, but it does not create it. I can learn to run fast, but I have a limited capacity: I'll never outrun a peak-performing Usain Bolt.

But do not be dismayed. Nobody needs us to be the best discerner; they need us to be better discerners. Greater than we were yesterday. And the route to developing discernment follows an easy formula. Perspective + Practice = Perfection.

Surely, you know I'm joking! However, we can develop discernment with practice, and it does require perspective, but we'll never be perfect. Let's review some anecdotal evidence from the previous chapter.

My mom and I may not have had hot water, *but our apartment wasn't crowded.* That's perspective. From Mr. Greg and Mr. Willie, I learned that I didn't need a lot of people, *just the right people.* That's perspective. To surround myself with the right people, I look for "right" behavior but measure it against individuality. *I must allow people to be themselves*—even if I don't like it. Then, I must choose my cadre. Sometimes I choose agreeable. Sometimes I choose disagreeable. That's discernment.

The only way to get this right is to stop fearing getting it wrong. Don't recklessly abandon caution, but don't allow fear to keep you from experimenting. If we don't experiment, how will we learn? Make it even more personal: *If I don't experiment, how will I learn?*

History can't teach us to look our circumstances in the eyes and decide what we trust, but our evaluated experience can. So, we must practice. Make decisions. Get some wrong. Get some right. Learn from them. Grow during the process.

I believe discernment is a gift from God. You may disagree. You may not believe in God. Regardless, you must acknowledge that fear can only protect a person when they have control, but faith protects even when life is out of control. [Pause: When you fight for something, do you fight fearing you'll lose it, or do you fight believing you can save it?] That's part of leadership: leading through chaos. In fact, that is leadership: ordering chaos. Circumstances *will* go haywire, and we will use our gift of discernment to restore order.

We all have the ability to decide; that's a gift. The size of our gift does not depend on us, but the extent to which we develop it does. I wholeheartedly believe that we can develop our skills far beyond what we can imagine. But that requires faith.

Back to the agenda: To become diligent leaders, we must become discerning leaders. To develop discernment, we must practice it, seek it, and understand that we will fail. Our goal is to *develop* leadership, and just like nobody runs a hundred-meter dash in under ten seconds on their first try, we won't have great discernment on our first try either. But we must try. We will improve, and that confident fearlessness will set us apart.

Quick Tips

> - We develop discernment when we experiment.
> - We must face our fears to experiment.
> - Faith will take us further than our fears.

My mother did not own a car when I was a child, but I got to ring the bell. My father did not live with us, but I received leadership training from men in the community. I grew up in the projects, but I didn't allow the projects to grow up in me. Things could have been worse. I never experienced the worst: life so despairing I couldn't see any way out.

Knee Deep

Discernment decides when to come and go; depression decides to stay in the hole.

    Back up. Step forward. Walk away. Lean into. Move around. Stay still. It'll change your perspective. Don't hold on so tightly. Think about this instead: "Take care then how you hear, for to the one who has, more will be given, and from the one who has not, even what he thinks that he has will be taken away."[5] I'll leave you with two questions so you can practice discernment. As a child, did I have, or did I have not? And how can you take from one who has not?

Shawn Foster

Quitting Time

I've gotta quit! I hate this man. I hope he dies. Please, God, not another. Please, God, I hate this man . . .

"Ten more, Shawn, I need ten more! Don't quit on me now! Be a man. Ten more!"

Sweat showered my eyebrows, stinging my eyes. I heard snickers, and I hit the ground again. *Ugh!* Up again. *Ugh!* Down again. *Ugh!*

"Seven more! Don't quit on me. Don't be weak. Are you weak, Shawn? Are you weak—"

I had begged my mom to enroll me in Pop Warner football. She scrounged up the money and made it happen, but I was the one who paid the price. I saw the coach's fiery eyes over his sweat-beaded nose, as he inhaled to give the whistle another blow. He barked instead.

"You're giving up, son. I can see it in your eyes. Don't be a quitter! Are you weak? Do you want to quit? Do you want your mommy?"

Yes! I want my mom. I hope she comes down here and beats your ass. I gotta quit. I can't finish. I—

My arm folded beneath me, my palms dented with pebbles. My facemask smacked the tough earth, blowing dirt in my eyes. I had three more to go. Only three more. I couldn't do it. *Ugh!*

Stay down. Stay down, pretend it's your arm. Scream!

"My wrist! I think I broke my wrist!"

"Let me see it."

I sat up, real tears mixed with false screams, looking at my cleats. I handed him my hand, crooked at the wrist.

"Don't be a baby, son. Crying is for sissies. You wanna be a sissy? Want some pom-poms? I can move you to cheerleading if that'll make

Knee Deep

you stop crying." He swaggered to the huddle, and I spoke to the unhearing air.

"I can't bend it. I think it's broken."

Please, God. Please come save me. Get me out of here. I promise I'll never play football again if you get me out of here.

Walking home, I cried from the football field to the front door. Why did that man hate me so much? What did I do wrong? I had to tell my mom as soon as I got home.

"How was practice?"

"I hate it! I want to quit! That coach is the meanest man in the world, Mom. I hate him."

"Son, we don't hate. You can hate the hurt, but we don't hate the man. That'll never change him; it'll only hurt you."

"Can I quit, please?"

I clutched my wrist, pushing it toward her face.

She grabbed it. "Does this hurt?"

"Yes! Everything hurts. Don't touch it."

"I'll tell you what, son. We'll tape your wrist up nice and tight tomorrow, so it doesn't hurt during practice."

I ran to my room and cried. She didn't understand how much that man hated me. I thought she would *protect* me, but she took his side. Adults always did that—took each other's side while the kids suffered.

Progress Update

We've discussed communication, leading and following, and practicing discernment. I have an assignment for you, but I'll set it up first. *Empathy* is a buzzword these days. We teach it as the panacea. But empathy can be dangerous. I've seen many parents make adult decisions with a childlike mentality. They empathized with the child and wallowed in their own childhood pain as a decision-making mechanism. That's incomplete. If we're going to apply empathy, then apply it all around. As you read the following anecdote—here's the assignment— empathize with the coach, Mom, and me. When we reach the end, I'll ask you to decide.

Shawn Foster

The following day, I dragged my feet while walking to practice. *I gotta figure out how to get out of this. Maybe I can run away. No, that's stupid. Maybe I can get kicked off the team for being late. I don't want to go anyway. I'll just—*

"Shawn Foster! Don't you ever disgrace my practice by showing up late again. That's fifty hit 'ems; I don't care if your wrist hurts or not. You hear me? Fifty!"

I cried before I hit the ground. I cried when I hit the ground. I cried walking home. I couldn't take anymore. When Mom later asked how practice went, I lied. "Good."

I had a few days' reprieve from practice, long enough to clear my head. I figured if the coach hated me, I could *make* him like me. I'd be his best player, do everything he said—even help him clean up.

I ran to practice, cleats clicking on sidewalks. I got there early and met the coach at his car.

"Coach, can I help you unload the gear? Need help carrying it to the field?"

He smiled. He'd never smiled at me.

"Sure thing, Shawn. Carry all this to the field. I'll be out there waiting."

Shoot. Now, he's using this to punish me. But I carried the pads, helmets, water bottles, etc., to the sidelines and arranged them as he instructed. I studied his mannerisms, spying for what I could mimic.

"Coach, want me to fill these water bottles?"

"Sure thing, Shawn. Thanks, son!"

It's working now. He's happy with me. I had killed him with kindness, heaped burning coals on his head. I knew he would take it easy on me now.

"Foster! You missed that block again! How old are you, son?"

"Eight, sir."

"Too scared for eight. Give me double. Sixteen hit 'ems."

"Yes, sir!"

Ugh! No tears. Determination. I would not lose to that man.

"You know what your problem is, son? All you want is glory. You don't block because you want to score touchdowns. I see it in your eyes. Well, today's your lucky day. Line up at tailback."

Knee Deep

I could outrun every kid on that team. When we did sprints, I smoked them all—not even close. This was my big chance! I only had to scratch my way outside the tackles, and I would be gone!

Jason, the quarterback, called the play. Handoff right to me. Easy money. I would hit the sideline and run straight up for the touchdown while the coach stared wide-eyed in disbelief. *Give me the ball!*

"Hit!"

Jason dropped back, stuffed the ball into my belly, and *BOOM!* Immediately, I got dropped by two defenders.

Now, this was Pop Warner football, third graders. Kids couldn't hit that hard, but when I took those two hits simultaneously, it put me down. I popped back up. I would show them.

Same result. Double-team tackle.

"Third down, Shawn. You gotta show me something on this one."

I shook the cobwebs free and looked right at him. "Yes, sir!" How could I—and then I knew. *Cut back!* My blockers sucked, so I needed to do something different. I'd seen Tony Dorsett do it hundreds of times. When defensive linemen got close, he shifted the opposite direction mid-stride and left the defenders in his dust. No problem. Cut back.

Jason slammed the ball in, knocking my breath out. I took one step, cut back, then two kids cradled me, knocking the ball high in the air. One of the defenders caught it and took off for a touchdown while I lay breathless on my back.

"Foster, you weenie! Don't you ever drop my football! You hear me? That's like a newborn baby! Don't you ever drop the football—"

Then he put me through the torture chamber: One hundred hit 'ems. Some parents got worried and expressed their concerns, but I saw him point to Mom when they pulled him aside. After the hit 'ems, I swallowed my tears, sucked in my belly, puffed my chest, and announced, "Coach, I'm done, sir. What's next?"

"Get back in there, Foster. Run the ball. Don't fumble."

Eventually, I broke off a few tantalizing runs, and even the coach couldn't deny my talent. But he didn't acknowledge it either.

GIVING PEOPLE WHAT THEY WANT FROM YOU DOESN'T ALWAYS CHANGE THEIR BEHAVIOR TOWARD YOU.

"Mom, you gotta let me quit. I hate football."

"What are you talking about? You have more touchdowns than the rest of the team combined. Why would you quit?"

"Because Coach hates me. He never congratulates me, and he smokes me every practice."

"What does that mean?"

"Do hit 'ems until smoke rolls out of my ears."

"Doesn't that make you better?"

"Mom, I can't do this anymore. Please, let me quit!"

"Shawn, you're not a quitter. You don't have to play next year, but you must finish this year. We don't quit when we're hurting; we quit when we're finished."

I hated those blankety-blank words. *We don't quit when we're hurting; we quit when we're finished.* We finished the season and won a trophy. I outscored the rest of the team and outplayed my practice self by ten to one. After the season, the coach's son, Roy, told me a secret.

"Shawn, you remember your first practice at tailback when you got stuffed in the backfield a million times?"

"Remember that time I ran for thirty-two touchdowns?"

"Listen! My dad told the defense your play while we were in the huddle."

"That ain't fair! Why would he—"

"I know. That's why I'm telling you. You didn't play badly. They knew the play the whole time."

"Man! Why would your dad do that? I never did nothing to him."

"I don't know."

"Does he hate me or something?"

"No way! He gave you the MVP award."

"Yeah, but he smoked me all the time."

"Maybe he wanted to deflate your head."

"I'd like to deflate his head."

I couldn't get our conversation out of my head. What had I done? That man *hated* me with a passion; it didn't matter what his son said. Although Roy was my friend, I got my parting shot in.

Knee Deep

"Thanks for telling me. I'm sorry for saying I wanted to deflate your dad's head."

"Don't worry about it."

"All those kids knew where I'd run?"

"Yeah."

"I still smoked those fools a few times!"

I played football for the next thirteen years. I never had a coach that mean again—not even close. Most coaches liked me. They said they found me "coachable." (Thanks, Mom.) I played tailback, kick returner, punt returner, and wide receiver when we got old enough to throw the ball downfield. Then I learned to kick. I won multiple MVP awards and championships and had the honor of being team captain. I loved the game, but I sure hated my first coach.

Quick Tips

> ➤ The price we pay today may be the investment of a lifetime.
> ➤ Children and adults are different: Treat them that way.
> ➤ A failure who gets up will eventually beat a winner who gets down.

One Saturday morning, a few years later, Mom and I went shopping. We needed standard stuff: milk, bread, cheese—nothing special. But I had high hopes we would pick out a treat. We'd spent that morning assembling gears, and I suppose grocery shopping was the reward. Mom worked for Rexham Corporation and assembled gears for extra money. She earned one cent per piece. I could say *we* earned one cent per piece since I assembled gears next to her, but I never saw any money! At that table, I learned that small margins make a big difference over time. We pieced those parts together and pinched pennies to string a living together. On Saturdays, we spent those pennies at the grocery store.

As we rounded the snack aisle, Mom pushed the cart while I pulled the items she called for. I ran right into Coach. I stumbled backward; my face flushed, jaw clenched, when—

"John, how are you? How's Betty?"

Shawn Foster

Mom knows his wife? What? I told her he was the meanest man on the planet— And then I saw it. Just above John's left shirt pocket, stitched into the fabric, were the words *Rexham Co.* He was my mom's coworker! She didn't know Betty; she knew *him*!

I fumed the entire walk home. "Mom! Why didn't you tell me you knew Coach? You made me play for him when he was being a—"

"Shawn, let me stop you right there. I knew John before you joined the team. He told me he was coaching a team, and I picked him for you. I told him to be hard on you. He didn't want to do it. I had to beg him every week to keep it up."

"Why? To 'toughen me up'? Teach me to be a man—all that bull people always talk about to Black boys?"

"Nope. Not at all. I told him to make you want to quit."

"Why?"

"Because we're not quitters, and we finish what we start. I didn't tell him to 'toughen you up.' I can do that on my own. I told him to make you want to quit because I know something you don't."

"Whatever."

"Don't you dare be disrespectful to me. Look at me. I told him to do it because the next thing you face will be tougher than the last."

Progress Update

We've just completed chapter five. You've likely considered Mom's decisions, my coach's decisions, my decisions, and hopefully some of yours. Did you empathize with everyone? Even the adults? Now's the time to practice discernment. If I had sustained a career-ending injury during the last game rather than winning MVP, the championship, and playing thirteen years of football, would Mom's decision have been a bad one?

Winning Time

"I'll see you Saturday."

"See you Saturday, Dad."

He descended the porch steps, walking toward his car. I hadn't grown up with him, so I was excited about seeing him the next Saturday. Would we go fishing, toss the football, work on cars together, whatever fathers and sons do? I'd recently moved from North Carolina to New Jersey. Mom moved me there to develop a relationship with my father and grow into a man. To start, I moved in with Grandma and Pop.

I had spent the summers with Grandma and Pop, so moving in didn't change my landscape too much. They lived in Pleasantville, so my greatest discomfort was transitioning from the warmer climate of North Carolina to the wet, colder temperatures of New Jersey. I'd spent the summers there but never winter. I didn't know the unpleasantries.

In the seventh grade, I hadn't much considered the weather. Yet I had considered two things about moving: Would I be the starting tailback, and would there be any cute girls? Would Pleasantville be pleasant for me?

The weather was different; the fashion was different; the people were different; the school was different; the traffic was different; the accents were different; and the food was very, very different. At Grandma and Pop's, the cuisine was much better than Mom's cooking, given that she didn't cook much. But in the community and at school, well, it repelled my stomach. Nobody ate fried okra, Bojangles didn't exist, tea tasted bitter, and people only ate cornbread with chili. Speaking of chili, they smothered their hot dogs in chili up there.

Shawn Foster

Seemed like a waste of good chili to me. Imagine a chili dog with unsweetened tea.

    I started school and fit in right away. As an outsider, I even got some undue attention from the girls, and nobody had to tell me twice to take advantage of that situation. Pleasantville had been pleasant so far. However, an opposite dynamic played out on the football field.

    We ran wind sprints. Tons of them. After hoofing through the first two, I heard a coach say, "Man, Foster can move!" Others heard, too. During our first practice, I shimmy-shook the defense out of their jockstraps and left them grasping their sides. That's all they caught that day: air and stitches in their sides. I cranked it up a notch. What could go wrong? I shredded the defense, and Pop saw it all. I'd soon be a Pleasantville Joker.

    But the joke was on me. On Friday, we had our first full padded practice. I blazed the field, shifting side to side, cutting back, and left the defense watching shoe bottoms. Our other tailback, Thomas, did pretty well also. He had good acceleration and moved through the holes fluidly, but he didn't have my breakaway speed. He got *caught*.

    After practice, he shoulder-checked me.

"Watch where you're going, Foster."

"What's going on?"

"Out there shaking your stuff like you're something special."

"I'm playing football."

"You think you're the best."

"I am the best. They can't catch me. Why's that a problem?"

"Your face is the problem. You keep showing out like you're—"

"Faster than everybody else on the team? Yeah . . . hey, what the—"

I saw orange splash from his cup into my eyes, and then two teammates pushed between us. After they pushed me back, yelling about being team players and all that, I walked away. It wasn't worth it. I wiped his sticky drink from my face and walked to Pop's car.

SOME BATTLES ARE NOT YOURS TO FIGHT.

I had that drink all over my shirt when I got in his car.

"I saw that, Shawn."

"Saw what?"

"That boy throw his drink on you. What's that about?"

"He thought I was showboating because I outran the whole team. I wasn't showboating, just playing my position."

"What do the coaches say?"

"Keep up the good work."

"Then that's what you do. Keep up the good work and ignore him."

"But he attacked me!"

"He's fighting the wrong battle."

"What do you mean?"

Pop grabbed the gear shift, pulled it into drive very slowly, and let out the brake. A full second passed, and he lightly pressed the accelerator, and we rolled casually toward the exit.

"He's defending his position, not himself."

"By attacking me?"

At the stop sign, he looked both ways and crept onto the road. Eventually, three or four cars lined up behind him, but he didn't adjust. He continued in a measured tone with governed pacing. "Well, it's understandable, but he's protecting something that ain't his. A position is a gift. Your character, that's something to defend, not a position."

"But I was defending myself."

"If you beat him up, what do you win?"

"My respect."

"Nope. Your respect comes from within. If you beat him up, what do you win?"

"I don't know. Tell me."

"Nothing. But you lose your character. Don't let him change your character."

LEADERS VALUE CHARACTER OVER SELF-JUSTIFICATION.

When we creaked into the driveway, my Uncle Eric greeted us, "I see you let Speedy drive."

"Yeah, I'm going to race Pop's station wagon later!"

"You think you can outrun it?"

"Sure thing—fastest kid on the team."

Shawn Foster

"Most humble, too. You probably could have run home quicker than riding with Speedy."

We were halfway up the drive when Pop stepped from the vehicle. He wiped the window with a rag and then walked out back. My uncle elbowed my side, so I followed Pop.

Pop's glasses nearly touched his project. He hunched over his workbench like he was spying on gnats.

"Pop, why are you so close?"

"Inspecting."

"It doesn't have to be perfect."

"I don't do things twice."

"Huh?"

"I'd rather do it right the first time—"

By then, I had already skedaddled toward the house. I ran inside, grabbed a snack, and told Grandma about practice. She paced around, wringing her hands.

"Grandma, what's wrong?"

"Honey, I forgot the toast. I let myself run out of bread."

In my mind, we could solve that problem in two seconds flat. "Why not ask Pop to run you to town?"

"I don't want to interrupt—"

I disappeared like socks in the dryer. "Pop, Grandma needs a ride to the store, but she doesn't want to interrupt you!" He grinned curiously, wiped his tools clean, and pocketed his hands. I ran back to the house. "He's coming. Don't worry."

"I wasn't worried. Just hated to bother him."

I showered and dressed so I didn't stink up the house. When I crossed through the living room, Pop opened the door for Grandma and told me goodbye. He followed her to the car, opened the door, and helped her in. I had never seen a man wait on a woman like that before, so I kept my eyes peeled. Come to think of it, I'm not sure Grandma had a license. I never saw her drive.

"Shawn, we'll be back in an hour. Don't eat the whole house while we're gone," Grandma called while Pop patiently started the car.

"I won't! I'll leave you half."

Knee Deep

I think the traffic signal changed twice before Pop turned the corner. I had no worries; I had things to do. I readied my bedroom, picked my outfit, and dreamt of Saturday. *Wonder what Dad has in store?* I busied myself until busyness burned out. A room can only get so clean. I heard the workshop calling; more specifically, I heard the workshop tools calling, so I went to check them out.

A circular saw fascinates young boys: the speed, the glimmer, and the ability to rip roughshod through boards. *Power does that.* I unleashed it and nearly ripped my fingers clean off, then jerked my hands away like the multitoothed spinning saw blade chased me. As it fell, I envisioned it bouncing against the floor and ricocheting through my shin. Luckily, the blade guard closed first.

I said a quick prayer. This was not a prayer of thanksgiving but a prayer of panic. Had I destroyed Pop's saw? The power cord had ripped from the outlet, and the saw bounced at least three feet high. I inspected it the way Pop would have, and I decided it passed the smell test.

Halfway back to the house, I remembered the key step to tool storage: Wipe it down, then put it up! I raced back, and I heard Pop's car. *No problem, I've got time.* I lived on borrowed time.

Time Out

Conventional wisdom says, "Character is what you do when no one is watching." I disagree. That's *environmental character*. A soldier under extreme duress may do something heinous when no one is watching. Environments change people. Besides that, character *develops*. Failure, when we're alone, teaches us discernment; it teaches us *when* we will fail, *when* we need people, and *when* to try again. That *builds* character. A more apt quote is, "Nothing is covered up that will not be revealed, or hidden that will not be known."[6] While character waxes and wanes, only the truth remains.

Time In

I met them at the car, and Grandma lamented. "I'm sorry we're eating after dark, Shawn. I'll have dinner ready in ten minutes." She hadn't realized I'd snacked the entire time while they were gone. *Isolation does that.* Or puberty! Pop opened her door, walked her into the home, then headed to the workshop. *Oh no!*

"Pop, dinner will be ready in ten minutes. Why are we standing out here?"

"Ten minutes? Your Grandma's been married to me for far too long to finish in ten minutes. We have time. Besides, I have a question. That boy on the team, the other tailback, what's his name again?"

"Thomas."

"What have you decided?"

"Uh—I've decided to let it slide."

"Good. Because he's got something you don't have."

"What?"

"He's got something to lose: his position. You have nothing to lose. Play like it."

The following morning, I woke up early. It was Saturday, and my dad was coming over. I waited. And waited. And waited. I moped around, kicking rocks and complaining, and then Pop took me to the workshop. We spent hours out there laughing; he told stories and taught me power tools. Then, the laughter stopped.

"Shawn, did you move the circular saw?"

"No, Pop."

"Then why's it hung backward?"

One deep breath. "I moved it."

"If I can't trust you to tell the truth, I can't trust you to be true."

I swallowed, accepting his advice. I had to swallow something else, too: My dad never showed up.

The following week, I played like I had nothing to lose and earned the starting position! Thomas didn't take it too hard. He moved to starting wide receiver. Then it was time for our first game. Mom never missed a game, but Dad missed it. He told Pop he'd make the next one, but I didn't trust him. That was new territory for me. When the next Saturday rolled around, Dad didn't show. I got angry. But I didn't stay angry. I understood.

Pop taught me to *play like I had nothing to lose.* I didn't have a close relationship with my dad; I didn't lose anything because he didn't show up. I never had it. Plus, I didn't know his circumstances. Why hold that against him? I had Pop. I quit pinning my hopes on Dad and took what I could get. And that was plenty. I abandoned preparing for Dad's arrivals, so when he showed up, I could be surprised. That worked for me. I played hard, unafraid to lose but seeking what I could gain.

At the end of the football season, we won the championship. During our celebration ceremony, I sat beside my new best friend, Thomas. I spent that year in Pleasantville hanging with Thomas and gleaning from Pop. I had faced something hard—feeling rejected by my father—but I didn't let it faze me. Honestly, I hardly noticed after the first few weeks because Pop filled the gap. And I barely missed my friends back home, either, because Thomas filled the gap. And the snow, well, it created some hellacious snowball fights. I could have wasted time bemoaning what I had lost, but I chose to revel in what I gained.

Later in life, I developed a friendship with my father. We never had that father-son bond, but we didn't need it. We were fine. I didn't judge him. I had already learned from Pop that if I couldn't trust people's words as true, I couldn't expect them to be true. I dropped those expectations. When I can't expect someone to be true, I don't hold it against them; I just don't give them things to keep.

However, Pop gave me the truth. I've kept everything Pop gave me, and I don't mean materially; I mean the lessons. I spent endless hours in that workshop, soaking in wisdom and learning to lead. Even now, when I get impatient and try to run everywhere all at once, I see Speedy, bent over that workbench, eyes on the prize, moving one smooth motion at a time. As I reflect, I realize his penchant for doing things right the first time usually led to him finishing first in the end. And I remember that every little thing I do right prepares me for when I'm at my wit's end.

Shawn Foster

Showing Up

Sometimes, we must deliver people to where they need to be; sometimes, we must walk them to the place. I experienced this near the end of high school. I didn't know where to go or how to get there. Showing up is nearly impossible when you don't know the meeting place. If I were graded on showing up, I would have received a DNA (Did Not Attempt).

I'd scored a stellar 705 on the SAT, skinning my teeth against the minimum acceptable requirement for collegiate student-athletes—by five points. Although I had a 2.6 GPA, I still might not graduate. I needed one class, one assignment even, to graduate. I teetered on failure's edge. Did I have college mapped out? I didn't even have Friday mapped out.

My football coach, Willy Young, had Friday mapped out. He had our plays mapped, our strategies mapped, and my path to Livingstone College all mapped out.

Livingstone is an HBCU (Historically Black College and University) in Salisbury, North Carolina, and its football program desperately needed a placekicker. To be candid, it needed a revolution.

The revolution began with Coach Rudy Abrams. He had connections, knew how to coach, and, more importantly, specialized in recruiting. Abrams dug deep in his Rolodex, leveraged his connections, and recruited the old-fashioned way. *He called his friends.* Fortunately for me, he and Coach Young were old friends.

WE DON'T NEED A LOT OF PEOPLE; WE JUST NEED THE RIGHT PEOPLE.

"Rudy, how's the new position treating you?"

Knee Deep

"Just wonderful! With a 1-9 record last year, the sky is the limit."

"Not if you lose that last game!"

"Ain't that the truth? To be honest, we need a soccer-style kicker. You know how hard it is to find a Black placekicker?"

"I have one."

"Enlighten me."

"And he's a senior."

"Does he have the grades?"

"Barely."

"The skill?"

"He can kick it a mile, and he's the fastest kid on the team."

"Send him."

"I'll bring him."

Coach Young called me to his office and told me about the opportunity. I knew nothing of Livingstone College or Salisbury. I looked them up myself. One win. Nine losses.

I went home and told my mom about the HBCU.

"I've got a tryout for a college team. Could mean a scholarship."

"Where?"

"Livingstone College in Salisbury."

"Where?"

"Coach Young knows where. He also knows the coach. He said I have a shot."

"Well, take it. Are they good?"

"1-9."

"You better get while the getting's good. Sounds like they need you. How are you getting there?"

"Coach said he'd take me." That's all the information Mom needed.

Coach pulled up early Friday morning and had something to say before I even got out the door.

"Don't go dressed like that, son. Put on something respectable. This is a college visit. We'll change into practice clothes on campus."

"Yes, sir."

I joined Coach Young, appropriately dressed, in the truck cab, and we followed the winding roads to Livingstone for fifty-five minutes. Just think: I had a future fifty-five minutes away, and I didn't know the way.

Often, we expect people to know the way when they don't. We call their lack of knowledge a lack of initiative. Coach could have said, "If he wants it bad enough, he'll find a way, but he didn't."

I'd never visited a college campus before, never walked among the trees, smelled the perfume wafting from the girls' dorms, heard the rowdy boys in Greek housing, nor laid eyes on a college goalpost from near midfield. If I had, I might have been more intimidated, but perhaps naivety served me well. Ironically, as a superintendent, I've persistently harped on planning, processes, and procedures, but as a teenager, I couldn't navigate a map.

The possibility of college was a new frontier for my family. If I ever made it there and found a way to finish, I'd be a first-generation college graduate. Thank God for Coach Young.

Coach Young soon introduced me to Coach Abrams. As football coaches are inclined to do, Abrams rifled through a minimalist campus tour and then rushed me to the field. After surveying its size, I set my mind on making the team. Yeah, the field loomed large, but something about it called to me—maybe an opportunity to be something more? I quickly changed into practice clothes and joined them, prepared to kick from the tee. But Coach Abrams didn't play that way. He played old-school football: Practice like you play.

A long snapper, quarterback, and a few offensive linemen greeted me. And people think I'm a stickler for process? We lined up about thirty yards out and warmed up. One snap, one quarterback hold, one kick through the uprights. Not too bad for my first college kick.

After warming up, we backed it up. I kicked from thirty-five, forty, and finally, forty-five yards out. My leg grew tired, and I'd more than proved myself, but Coach Abrams wanted a fifty-yarder. Back then, very few high school kids kicked from fifty yards out, but I'd nailed some in practice. What I hadn't done was kick a fifty-yarder on a college field with my future on the line. I wiped my sweaty hands on my towel, backed up, and gave the holder the nod.

"Hike."

The snap sailed high, but like a receiver, he snatched it from the heavens and placed it, and I tried to kick it to the moon . . .

The somber drive home excited me less than the drive out did. Coach Young intimated I'd get the call, but I wasn't so sure. Trust but verify. I dumped the details on Mom when I got home, but I had bigger fish to fry: I still needed to graduate! And that one was a whopper. As I heard an elderly gentleman once say, "The picture of that fish weighed fourteen pounds!"

Fishermen often dub trophy fish they've seen but not snagged with larger-than-life nicknames: Leviathan, Tank, Moby, Monster, and even *Latin*. I needed one lousy grade to graduate, and a dead language teacher was my *ianitor*. Don't ask me what that means; I looked it up because, fortunately for me, I had a Latina secret agent named Melba in my class.

Melba and I met in middle school, and we've stayed friends ever since. When I returned from New Jersey, we picked up where we left off, and our relationship grew. We had zero romantic inclination, but we always had a good time. Melba played the big sister role.

"Shawn, have you finished your history homework?"

"Maybe."

"Shawn, are you going to the student council meeting?"

"Probably not."

"Shawn, are you—"

"Melba!"

Although we weren't interested in each other, she knew about my Romantic language woes; she'd seen my Latin grade. I fished for a monster with a five-pound test line. My Latin teacher threw me some bait: "Complete your Latin journal, and you'll graduate." The day after we submitted our journals, he patted my shoulder. "Good job on that journal. You got an A." Now, I'd come to class fully prepared to fail, ready to try my negotiation skills, but it was unnecessary. I looked at Melba's sly grin.

That Saturday, Coach Young drove over with a fistful of paperwork to sign: a full-ride athletic scholarship to Livingstone College because everyone knew I couldn't get there on academics alone! Coach coached me up, then fed me to the wolves.

Quick Tips

Shawn Foster

> ➢ Motivate the uninspired. Train the unknowing.
> ➢ Lead the way for those who don't know the way.
> ➢ Befriend leaders and follow their lead.

College football moves at an entirely different pace than high school football. Everyone is big, strong, and fast. All the football players have chips on their shoulders—many were high school stars. And when the whistle blows, if you don't see your momma in the stands, well then, pucker up, Buttercup, because a 250-pound man who runs a 4.6 40-yard dash is headed straight for you with bad intentions.

That created another problem for me. My mom had told me, "The next thing you face will be tougher than the last," and I thought I'd already faced that in New Jersey, where I was the new kid on the block and faced football without my mom. However, in New Jersey, I had Pop, and I didn't kick field goals in jam-packed rival college stadiums with a scholarship on the line, playing for a new coach with his career on the line.

All through Pop Warner, middle school, and high school, my mom never missed a game, except for my time in New Jersey. Although she worked two jobs and had no car, she always showed up. However, the biggest game of my life thus far finally outstretched her limits. No way she could attend a game two hours away on a Saturday, so I had to take what I could get. I turned to the Bible.

Before the game, while dressing in the locker room, I raced to the nearest stall and vomited. Before fully exiting the stall, I charged back in and threw up again. I grabbed my secret weapon. I didn't read it; I shoved it atop my thigh pad for good luck! Then we took the field.

I sized up our opponent, and even their waterboy looked faster than me. I kicked it into the end zone, but their returner ran it out from eight yards deep! The collisions rivaled those of Mack trucks, but by the grace of God, I survived the kickoff and didn't get too pummeled. Did I mention I was the kicker?

Coach Abrams knew his stuff, and we put on an offensive Masterclass, driving the field in a few plays and punching in a touchdown. I trotted onto the field to kick the automatic extra point.

I missed it.

Knee Deep

I looked in the stands. No Mom. I looked to the sidelines: one pissed-off head coach. I survived the next kickoff and watched the other team one-up our Masterclass and punch the ball in with fewer plays. Their extra point sailed perfectly through the uprights.

We took the field. Same result. Offensive drive. Touchdown. Extra point—*missed.*

WE DON'T QUIT WHEN WE ARE TIRED; WE QUIT WHEN WE ARE FINISHED.

I'd never wanted to quit so badly. I'd take my third-grade coach twice over again to avoid that pressure. Coach Abrams read me the riot act, and everybody on the team sent the same message with their eyes: *Put up or get out!* I wanted out.

I stormed the field to warm up again when my Bible slid down my thigh, and while I readjusted it, I heard familiar voices. Not the mental ones telling me to put up or get out, but the kind that cheered for me from the stands and sounded like angels. Mom and my aunts had driven two hours to this away game, our season opener!

Suddenly, the other team seemed pint-sized. *I'd smoke their middle linebacker. They can't hang with me.* I got a little taller, filled out the shoulder pads. *Put me in, Coach!* And he did. After we scored our next touchdown, I split the uprights with an extra point. Ten minutes later, I knocked a field goal through. Back and forth we went, push and pull, offensive score, defensive stop until time ran thin.

We only had one choice. With thirteen seconds remaining, down by two points—two missed extra points—I had my redemption shot, and it wasn't a chip shot. I lined up for the kick. I wiped my sweaty hands on my towel, backed up, and gave the holder the nod.

"Hike."

The snap sailed high, but like a receiver, he snatched it from the heavens, placed it, and I tried to kick it to the moon! The ball bounced off the left upright and fell behind the post. The kick was good! Just like that fifty-yarder at tryouts.

The Kick Was Good

Shawn Foster

Measure me, not by your presuppositions but against my purpose. Coach Abrams gave me a scholarship to pass classes and kick field goals. Sure, knowing how to get to college, class, and the field was prerequisite knowledge, but measuring me against that wastes potential: yours and mine. Often, we presuppose others can do our basics because they can do their bravura.

Coach Young solved that problem by teaching me. He showed me the way by leading the way and ensuring I got there. Then, and only then, did he back off. But not before he showed the way.

Quick Tips

> - Expectations without explanation are presumptions.
> - Expectations without communication are silent wishes.
> - Expectations without training are childhood dreams.

The *lives*-changing kick was good because neither coach judged me on my college-finding ability but on my field goal-kicking ability. I wrote *lives*-changing because that kick changed more than one. I found a place in college, eventually graduated, gained employment, met my wife, had two kids, and led various schools in various disciplines because one coach led the way and the other kept me on the path.

Too often, we judge others based on what *we* think they should know rather than judging the work they are purposed to do. Let that sink in. *What we think they should know.* Shouldn't they know this already? I thought she would know. Who doesn't know that? They should have known.

Here's a question: Who *should* have shown me how to get to college? Someone who'd never been, or the persons who had? Again, too frequently we judge people on what we presuppose they have learned—our expectations of them based on our experiences.

Still don't believe me? Next time you attend an event, check your manners at the door and see if you're invited back. Watch how people judge you for manners they think you should know. Then ask yourself: When do *I* judge others for what *I* think *they* should know?

Knee Deep

Leaders, we must ensure they know and know how.

Sometimes, we must deliver people where they need to be; sometimes, we must walk them to the place. And sometimes, we must teach them to stay.

Shawn Foster

Staying Time

Time stopped in the trailers. They backed another in. I sat for a hot minute while it hit the dock, and the other two employees nearly ripped the hinges off. The humidity rolled out, knocking me to the floor. I stood and the room spun, but I walked into the trailer . . .

My freshman year of college, I had a lot of fun, and my grades reflected it. I had a 1.5 GPA but several good excuses: I was a first-generation college student, a student-athlete, had barely graduated high school, and whoever designed the college campus must have been nuts!

We had separate dorms. Livingstone didn't have coed dorms. We had dorms divided by gender, and right in the middle of campus, we had Greek plots and the cafeteria. My dorm touched the bottom of the hill.

Walk *up* the hill with me to class. Start at Dancy, an all-male dorm. Linger at Harris, the female freshman dorm, and hear their playful laughter. Enter the Horseshoe and watch everybody mingle, planning the next big event. Taste lunch in the cafeteria. Feel the breeze as we pass Goler, another female dorm. Do you smell it? It's another shot at failure: Babcock Hall—an all-girls dorm. Arrive at Price, where we'll have our first class.

Count with me: one, two, three female residencies, the eating and meeting place, and then where we had classes. I woke up with every class-attending intention, but by my trek's end, I invariably got distracted. I earned everything I had coming: academic probation, a threatened scholarship, and my licks from the Omega Psi Phi Fraternity Inc. Then, I joined Mom at home for summer school.

Like all good leaders do, she challenged me when I needed it most.

"Shawn, since you had such a great time at Livingstone, you'll work full-time while you finish summer school."

"Yes, ma'am."
"Luckily for you, you don't need to search for employment."
"Why's that?"
"I know the right person. My friend works at Kmart Distribution, and he has a job for you."
"Great!"
"You'll be loading trucks."
"No problem."

As a college athlete with superior skill and stamina, I didn't fear manual labor. I'd survived more two-a-days than I could count. And it was good money. It couldn't be that hard to show up and load trucks.

We powered through that first truck, and I thought I might die. I nearly passed out. No water, sweat pouring to the floor, and my coworkers out-loaded me two-to-one. When we finished the first truck, I thought we'd take a break. I thought wrong. When one door closed, another door opened, and I walked into another human sweatbox.

At the day's end, I contemplated quitting, but I remembered: *We don't quit when we're tired; we quit when we're finished*. I returned. We loaded more trucks. At the day's end, I contemplated quitting. The cycle repeated until the fourth day's quitting time, and I'd had it. So, I quit.

Know When to Quit; Know When to Stay

I can hear it now. *You quit after four days! You're a hypocrite.*

Baloney! I said I want us to become discerning leaders. I made a discernment decision. *I can't do manual labor the rest of my life, so I better get my butt back in school and pass all my classes with straight As.* That's precisely what I did. I finished summer school with As, kept my scholarship, and made a 4.0 for the rest of my undergraduate career.

Progress Update

We've reached an inflection point. Was it a defining moment when I decided to work harder mentally than I worked physically? I could reflect upon that decision as a watershed moment. Was it a moment, or did my aggregate experiences teach me not to quit? Don't. Quit. School.

Shawn Foster

> The inflection point is where we discern if we're determined or if we're destined.

You decide. When faced with the decision, I'd already given my best, and my best wasn't good enough. I could continue to give my best loading trucks, or I could give my best at school—the place I'd originally committed to giving my best.

I returned to my original intention. I'm not indicating that I made the right decision; I'm indicating that I made *a* decision. *Sometimes, any decision is better than no decision.* What's yours?

My anecdote about quitting Kmart is precisely that—an anecdote. It could be a cautionary tale or a wise omen. Either way, it was my experience, and *every experience doesn't determine a right or wrong, but it does determine a direction.* I decided that I was headed in the wrong direction, so I did an about-face and stayed in school. It was staying time.

Was I a hypocrite? Did I wimp out? Did I dishonor my mom and her friend? You be the judge. I'm okay with it.

Quick Tips

> ➢ As leaders, we must align people with experimental hardships. (Thanks, Mom!)
> ➢ As leaders, we must seek solutions.
> ➢ As leaders, we must know when to quit or continue.

Finding a Way

I needed a job. As a graduating senior from Livingstone, I still didn't have a plan. *Learning takes time.* In my case, that meant a lot of time! As I've said before and I'll say again, I don't need a lot of people; I just need the right people. Dr. Curtis Tyrone Gilmore Sr. was that person.

He and Dr. James "Patch" Talley, the first African American mayor of Spartanburg, South Carolina, lectured our football team as guest motivators. They had my attention. They spoke well. They were successful. They had purpose. And, there was something more.

Dr. Gilmore had recently vacated his position as Grand Basileus (national president) of Omega Psi Phi Fraternity, Inc. and he also graduated from Livingstone. We had a connection. I'm a lucky guy, and that connection opened the door for a conversation.

"Dr. Gilmore, I need a job."

"I see you're not shy."

"Not in the slightest."

"We have positions in Spartanburg. Come visit us, and I'll set up an interview."

"Are you going back today?"

"Sure am."

"Can I ride with you?"

"Son, you aren't shy! How will you get back to Livingstone?"

"Dr. Gilmore, if you take me with you, I'll find a way."

"You've got a deal."

I rode with Dr. Gilmore to Spartanburg and interviewed, then hitched, bummed, and bused my way back. In my four years at college, I hadn't learned to plan, but I had learned to find my way. That's growth.

Shawn Foster

Coach Young had taken me to Livingstone, but I'd learned to trust myself to get where I needed to be. That's confidence. I made the right gamble.

Two weeks later, I got a call from Dr. Eubanks. Dr. Gilmore had put in a good word, and Dr. Eubanks' district adjoined Dr. Gilmore's. I grew more connected by the moment.

"Shawn, I've got an opening at our alternative school."

"I'll take it, but I'm not an education major."

"It's an aid position while you work on your licensure."

"I'll be there."

I arrived, and it was hell on wheels. Even the law enforcement officer had backup! Spartanburg County is divided into seven school districts, and the alternative school enrolls students from all seven. I'll spare you the gritty details, but you can imagine students from seven districts attending one alternative school. Teenagers with raging hormones who've been displaced from their school for violence, substance abuse, sexual misconduct, bullying, and general defiance of authority—perpetually. I saw things there I wished I could unsee.

I loved it. I'm not sadistic; I got it. The students didn't fit. The mold didn't work. So why transfer them to another school and give them the same old thing that frustrated them in the first place? We didn't. I learned very quickly: *Behavioral success creates academic success.* Students who don't feel environmentally safe because of *the probability* of nearby misbehavior fail to be successful, as well as students who don't adapt environmentally and therefore misbehave.

I found a way to be successful—a way for us all to be successful. I went to all seven superintendents and pitched the idea of a summer boot camp.

Progress Update

We're over a quarter of the way through the book. Let's check your pulse. Reread this sentence: "I went to all seven superintendents and pitched the idea of a summer boot camp." What jumps off the page? That's not rhetorical, either.

Knee Deep

> I'm not implying anything; I'm indicating something. I had direct access to seven superintendents before I even had a teacher's license. I could complain about being stuck at an alternative school, or I could . . .

We started the summer boot camp. Our law enforcement officers ran it. We had fatigues, physical training, skill-based training, and behavioral rehabilitation. I handled the in-school suspension portion and acted as the counselor. We had such great results that we ran the camp as a year-long program.

Certain behaviors warrant expulsion, like bringing a loaded weapon to school. Certain behaviors are borderline, like vandalizing school property. In lieu of expulsion, students could enroll in the boot camp academy and stay in school. Now, for those not in education, how do you persuade a student who hates school to stay in school and go to boot camp?

You don't.

Let me whisper in your ear: Students who have behavior problems at school often have behavior problems at home, too. I'm not being condescending; I'm being logical. We didn't persuade the students; we talked to the parents. Parents don't want to deal with behavior problems all day or leave their problem child at home unattended, so the boot camp sold itself. It provided a solution. We made a way when there was no way. We became *opportunistic*.

Leaders Are Opportunists

I asked AI to provide terms describing individuals who take advantage of others. Here's what I got: *opportunist*, manipulator, exploiter, predator, user, schemer, swindler, parasite, freeloader, and grifter. It paired opportunists with predators and parasites. *Merriam-Webster's Dictionary* defines *opportunists* as "Taking advantage of opportunities as they arise: such as exploiting opportunities with little regard to principle."[7] Opportunists sound evil! I must disagree.

In leadership, we laud taking advantage of teachable moments. When I returned from my freshman year of college, Mom saw an opportunity. She saw me deviating from an opportunity-filled future and gave me one that felt like a dead end. She *knew* me. Given the opportunity to suffer heatstroke in a dust-filled trailer or return to playing college football and hanging with coeds, which would Shawn choose? But she didn't give me the choice; she gave me the taste. I needed skin in the game. Mom saw the opportunity, phoned her friend, and let me experience the pain. I have the utmost respect for labor-intensive jobs, but given the choice, I choose school!

Mom didn't exploit her friendship or manipulate her principles. She enacted them. Her friend knew I could quit or stay. Nobody had a crystal ball foretelling my future, but Mom made an opportunity-based decision. Either outcome served her purpose: Her son had employment and could learn a lesson—a win/win. She took advantage of a teachable moment, snagged it from the sky, and put it right on me!

Being an opportunist is considered pejorative, but it's not. You're not a grifter if you see opportunities and take action—you're a leader. We all know some leaders have malevolent intentions while others have philanthropic ones. There is a defining difference between the two, and practicing that difference makes the difference.

Again, *practicing* the difference makes the difference. Good leaders practice seeing opportunities that benefit all. Bad leaders practice seeing opportunities that only benefit them. They only consider all when all benefits them. But the practice makes the difference. Knowledge is not enough. Knowing better does not equal doing better. Just because we know the difference between taking a Tootsie Pop from a baby to save her teeth and stealing it to eat it ourselves doesn't mean we will make the right choice. So, there's a hole we must dig, a tree we must plant, and roots we must nurture to practice being an opportunist.

Interestingly, when I queried AI for a descriptive term for individuals who opportunized *while* maintaining good moral character, what do you think the answer was?

Discerning.

Good leaders solve problems, initiate change, and create growth through opportunities, and good leaders embody discernment while they take action. We consider the moral implications. We evaluate the cost on others. We analyze the damage. But we don't rest on our laurels. We take the moral high ground, even if it costs our comfort or our position. We are opportunistic. And we practice discernment.

But *discernment* rings hollow to those who don't trust their judgment. We need a building block first. To build our character so we trust our judgment, we need a practice everyone can do—an all-skate. Everyone can serve, and the way we make a way is through practicing *service*.

Shawn Foster

Service Is the Journey; Leadership Is the Goal

Serving others builds *our* character. Dr. Gilmore gave me an opportunity. He served it up but didn't force-feed it to me. I did the work. I served the students and parents at the alternative school. I took the opportunity to give students actionable ways to dig, plant, and grow their character roots through the boot camp program: Practice respect, dress appropriately, move your mind and body, and serve others. The parents, staff, and students enjoyed the fruit. So did the rest of society. The boot camp infused service-oriented practice into the students' days rather than invoking another punishment when punishments had failed. So, how do we learn to serve?

I have a three-step approach to building a service mindset that builds opportunistic leaders guided by character.

3-Step Service Builder

1. Dig the hole.
2. Plant the tree.
3. Nurture the roots.

Dig the Hole

Yes, you can dig the hole. Yes, you can become service-oriented. Yes, it's a skill to learn, not a birthright. Yes, you must say yes. If you're new to serving, if you haven't developed a service mindset, you can become service-minded by saying yes. And, you must say yes often. I'm talking about over-the-top overkill here.

Think about an infant. We wrap them in blankets and strap them in car seats backward to protect them. We *overprotect* them. Culturally, we rationalize these steps as standard protection, and we make it a law. Think about it. We hold them in our laps on airplanes, carry them in our arms descending stairs, and place them in random stranger's arms (Santa Claus) for pictures. But in the car, we overprotect them. Why?

During a rapid growth phase, we overdo it! Look into radical societal changes—revolutions, if you will. The eccentric leaders pushed the envelope. Sometimes, change requires us to overdo it. If we want to become service-minded, we must overdo it, especially at the start.

We say yes so much it hurts. We should experience "yes fatigue," just like we experience muscle fatigue. Let's work out. And then we'll adapt. We'll learn discernment and know how to use a yes for a no.

I get invited to events constantly when I already have a full plate. How do I say yes when I need to say no? I let my yes become the no. Ask me to go out to dinner when I already have plans with Tanya. You won't get a no; you'll still get a yes. I'll respond with something like: "Yes, I'd love to come on a night when I don't already have dinner plans with Tanya." I'd already said yes to Tanya, so I can't say yes to you. I'm not rejecting you; I'm keeping a commitment.

Do it. Become a "yes if" person and not a "no because" person. Become a person who shows up extra, often too much, takes the invitation, doesn't give no for an answer, and says yes to opportunities.

We can't maintain that posture forever, but for a little while—long enough to expose the dirt and dig in deep—we must say yes frequently enough to dig a hole. Then, we fill it in. We stuff that serving hole with a giant tree. Then, we'll see its roots grow.

Plant the Tree

To plant the tree, we must build general service practices into our lives, so we can spot service opportunities and position ourselves to lead. Let's make it easy and grab the low-hanging fruit first.

Almost all companies, programs, and people seek volunteers. Ample volunteer opportunities surround us. Often, we can't keep people from kicking our door in, begging us to help. So, stop. Stop keeping people from kicking the door in and start volunteering. Find an animal shelter, go to Habitat for Humanity, or seek a place of worship. Do something. Get involved. Volunteer and watch those roots hit the ground.

After volunteering becomes second nature, create service opportunities by building a service habit. Pick something you do to serve others and carry the materials necessary. I know a gentleman who helps people experiencing car trouble. If there's a roadside car with a driver, he stops and offers assistance. He keeps tools and a jack with him. He's prepared. I know another who carries an umbrella. When it rains, he walks people from the car to the store or vice versa. Both have created opportunities to serve through service habits, and that straightens the tree in the hole.

As if that weren't enough, we must fill the hole with dirt, and we do that through invitation. Invite opportunities to serve by inviting people to spend time with you. If we invite someone to our home, we feel obliged to serve. We clean up. We offer them a drink. We shift into service mode. Hospitality imbues us. We can also fill the hole by inviting others to events, dinners, parties, etc., but nothing supports the servant spirit quite like inviting someone into our space. We tamp in the tree. And then we invite some more!

Nurture the Roots

Inviting others to serve with us fertilizes our servant roots. Enlisting others invites accountability into our lives. If we snatch our friend to accompany us when we help a neighbor build a patio, we create accountability. We present ourselves as servants and set an expectation not only for ourselves but also for the hearts of others.

With accountability comes opportunity. Alongside others, we can reorganize kitchens or repaint park benches. Whatever the service is, when we invite others, we create self-accountability, and we surround ourselves with service-minded people—or people on their way to becoming service-minded. As the old adage says, "Show me your friends, and I'll show you your future." Our opportunities to serve abound. We have more opportunities, we see more opportunities (as do our friends) and service seeps into our character—fertilizing our roots.

That's when we can see clearly: When service becomes who we are, and we no longer look for it but live it. It's a nonnegotiable, an automated response like blinking. We no longer ponder and wonder; we do because we are. As Zig Ziglar often said in his *Strategies for Success* series, "You've got to *be* before you can do, and you've got to do before you can have." You've got to be service-minded before you serve from character, and you've got to serve from character before you have positive leadership. After we fertilize our roots and develop a service-minded character, the world becomes our oyster, and we capture the pearl of great price.

THE MORE WE GIVE, THE MORE GOD GIVES US TO GIVE.

Journey to Leadership

Serving creates leadership opportunities. If we're looking to lead, if that's the end goal, service is the pathway. Service-oriented people build networks, receive opportunities, and create trust.

Think of the most well-connected people. Immediately, we might consider CEOs, entertainers, and superstars. But take a moment to inspect. Hunch over, as Pop did, and get close to the individuals who seem to "know everybody." What do you see? They're service-minded. They invite. They engage. They create. Who do you know who's highly networked? Is that person service-minded?

Not to skip the superstars, I heard an anecdote on ESPN's *The Last Dance,* where Scott Williams indicated that Michael Jordan invited him over for dinner many times when Williams joined the Bulls. Willams had lost his parents a few years earlier, and Jordan said, "Juanita is cooking spaghetti tonight. Come over for dinner!"[8] What could Jordan gain from Williams? Why not *take* Williams to dinner? Why not let Williams buy his own dinner? He played NBA basketball, for crying out loud—he could afford it. Who is more connected, more recognizable, and more of a leader than Michael Jordan? But he served.

When we serve, we get more opportunities to lead. Another adage says, "When you want something done, do it yourself." Again, baloney! A different adage says, "If you want something done, ask a busy person to do it." The adage doesn't relate solely to busyness; it relates to getting things done. Good leaders get things done, but they don't do it all themselves. They get opportunities to get things done because they know how. They know whom to employ and whom to avoid. And by virtue of getting things done, more opportunities come their way, and they ascend the leadership ladder. Most importantly, they develop a reputation: a reputation for getting things done. You can trust them.

Ultimately, good leaders develop trust, and practicing servanthood builds that bridge. With time, people trust leaders, so when circumstances go awry, as they often do, people defend the leader. They want the leader to remain the leader, and they'll fight for it. Imagine if the same individual you infuriated at one point fought for your honor at another. Not because you gave them what they wanted but because you did what you said. You remained trustworthy. That's leadership! And it doesn't happen by accident; it occurs with the repeated practice of servanthood—a servant lifestyle.

Whom Do We Serve?

We serve those in need, then those in want. This doesn't mean we prioritize one class over another; it means we make discerning decisions. Everyone needs help sometimes, so helping a billionaire tie her shoe isn't less worthy than helping a four-year-old. However, if the billionaire continues calling us over, and she has the resources to get it done while the four-year-old doesn't, what should we do?

I included that question to see if you'd overdo. Remember, to build a service mindset, we must overdo. But also remember, we don't do all things in the same manner. What applies to one does not apply to all, and what's wise today may be tomorrow's downfall.

As humans, we have an infinite capacity to overdo. I'll write *leaders serve*, and within a month, someone will serve himself to death. That's an impoverished mentality: *I need more. It's never enough.* And that's the mentality we want to avoid because it kills us and them. If we overserve, we burn out. If we overserve those for whom it's never enough, *they worsen.* So, balance service with need before want. Everyone wants to be served, but who needs it?

Leaders Build Leaders

We must build up good leaders for the next generation. We know we're good leaders when we build leaders who even we would follow. Everyone benefits.

    I led my college football team to a championship as a wide receiver, placekicker, and team captain. At the alternative school, I gained a network, opportunities, and trust. I shifted from an intervention specialist to a guidance counselor, then transitioned into an assistant director, and later took an assistant principal position at Paul M. Dorman High School.

    The remainder of my career has overflowed with so many leadership opportunities, and it's been life-giving, albeit at times heart-wrenching. We'll begin with one of my most life-giving experiences in leadership. During my first assistant principal position, I experienced the proudest moment of my leadership journey when I watched a loose-lipped boy become a life-giving young man.

Shawn Foster

Showing Up 2.0

He had it in him. As the kids would say, "His words were fire," and they almost burnt his butt up. A natural-born leader, both gregarious and incorrigible, Jamaal Rashon Dukes had it coming, and someone had to give him the business—me.

Don't skip a beat. I know I wrote "natural-born leader," and I'm checking your pulse. Did you catch it? I opened this memoir by suggesting leaders are both born and built, but then I just claimed my proudest moment came from watching a "natural-born leader." I don't know if Jamaal split the womb that way or developed it over time, but when I met him, he could already lead. He just led people the wrong way. I had to redirect; I had to lead him where he needed to be, to take him to the place, and then I let him fail.

Paul M. Dorman High School boasted the second-largest enrollment in South Carolina during my tenure. Imagine a school teeming with 2,000–2,500 squirrely teenagers all vying for attention. Even those who appeared to dodge attention craved it. Dale Carnegie wrote in *How to Win Friends and Influence People,* "The desire to be important is the deepest urge in human nature."[9] In my words, everyone wants to be important to someone, and most stop at nothing to achieve it. Jamaal exemplified this sentiment every passing hour.

As a newly minted assistant principal, one of the duties that befell me was directing discipline. Over 75 percent of Paul M. Dorman's *teenagers* hailed from economically disadvantaged homes, which include single-parent homes, transient and homeless students, foster care, etc. We'll say discipline itself was a full-time job. I became well acquainted with student discipline.

Knee Deep

Jamaal Dukes greeted me in the hallways. We didn't meet in the office after a discipline referral; we met when he spotlighted me to other students.

"Hey! Have you met Dr. Foster? He's my mentor."

"I'm not your mentor."

"There goes my mentor on his way to bus duty."

"I'm not your mentor."

"Dr. Foster always be hustling kids to class: He's my mentor."

"I'm not your mentor. But I will be. Here's the deal: You keep saying, 'He's my mentor, he's my mentor,' so if you want me to be your mentor, you must run for student council."

"Say what? That's not me. I'm not—"

"You want me to be your mentor or not? I didn't say you must win. I said you must run."

I saw the wheels turning. He quickly evaluated how he could take advantage, and as I figured, his advantage meant extra attention, so he took the bait.

"I'll do it."

"You've got yourself a mentor."

Jamaal clowned around constantly—a real knucklehead. And people watch knuckleheads. They're like a police chase: We sit on edge, waiting to see what will happen next, knowing it probably won't be good, but it will be entertaining. Students followed him. He led, but I wanted to see what direction he'd lead after the election.

He won. I figured he would; he'd already pocketed much of the student body. He joined the student council, which had several responsibilities, including designating who made the morning announcements. Guess who they picked? Yep. Jamaal Dukes.

Again, everyone sat on edge, wondering what he'd do. Before I allowed it, I mandated he write a script for my approval, and then he could Marla Gibbs his way into the Student Council Hall of Fame. He did brilliantly. He spoke in an old lady's voice to captivate his audience, and it worked. To say the students loved it understates the truth.

Now, I hawkeyed him because we had an older African American teacher, Ms. Donna Mays, and I didn't want him impersonating her—that would have been disrespectful. Jamaal knew his limits, so he didn't

Shawn Foster

cross the line. We had many older African American staff members, but I especially protected Ms. Mays. *Sometimes, you can't see it coming, but you know you're about to get hit.*

Jamaal preferred the right cross, a boxing maneuver where the boxer offsets his opponent with a deft left jab followed by an immediate right. The right sneaks in behind the left, while the other boxer can't see it—*pop, Pop*! Or, in this case, *pop, Drop*!

The Sadie Hawkins dance was upcoming, and Jamaal announced the invitation. Ladies invite gentlemen to a Sadie Hawkins dance, so it flips the script on traditionalism. That fit Jamaal perfectly. Do you see it coming?

Jamaal got on the mic. "Ya'll come on out Friday night to the Sadie Hawkins Dance where Ms. Donna Mays's going to drop it like it's hot on Mr. Burgess, and we'll dance the night away. Y'all know that the girls must invite the guys, so, ladies, make sure you invite your gentlemen before time runs out and you're—"

Mr. Burgess burst through my doorway. I looked up from my desk into his round eyes, "Yes, Mr. Burgess?"

"Did you hear that?"

"Yes, Mr. Burgess. I heard it. I'm writing the discipline referral now, and then I'll go get him."

"Dr. Foster, he can't get away with insulting our integrity. You took him under your wing; you fix it."

"I'll fix it."

I suppressed my laughter beneath his bulging eyes, but when he left the office, I let loose. I think I heard the door slam. Then I got Jamaal.

"Jamaal, do you know what you did?"

"Yes."

"What do you have to say?"

"It was wrong."

"You know what I have to do?"

"Suspend me."

"Suspend you for ten days and recommend you for expulsion. Defamation of character. It's a serious offense. I gave you a shot, and you disappointed me."

"I understand, sir."

"By the way, they weren't the only two whose character you defamed. You understand?"

"I understand."

I understood, too. I turned it back on Jamaal. I didn't bring my emotional baggage and explain how deeply he wounded me, etc. He hadn't. Sure, he disappointed me, but, more importantly, he defamed his own character—he disappointed himself. That's the point. I couldn't take on his issues; I had to push them back where they belonged. Jamaal needed to deal with Jamaal.

Jamaal had issues at home, too. I won't discuss them, but he had reasons behind his attention-seeking behavior. I knew that, his mom knew that, and he knew that. Despite his reasons, I had to do what I had to do.

Leaders do what's hard, even when it breaks their hearts.

Shawn Foster

Showing Up 3.0

I hope you reacted the same way the student body did: They went nuts. They lost their ever-loving minds. But as you know by now, *we don't lead by what's popular but by what's right*—what's right for everybody.

A few days after the fiasco, Jamaal's mother joined me to discuss his future in the district and if he'd even have one. See, expulsion can be permanent . . .

"Ms. Beverly, I'm recommending Jamaal for expulsion. He defamed the character of a highly tenured teacher and a highly tenured assistant principal. We can't allow that behavior to go unpunished."

"I understand, Dr. Foster, and I'm thankful for all you've done for Jamaal."

"Now, Ms. Beverly, as his mother, I need you to appeal."

"I'm sorry."

"I need you to appeal my decision to the principal. Here's what you'll say—"

Jamaal made a mistake, a costly one, but a mistake that aligned with his character. Not only his character as a knucklehead but as a leader. He wanted people to follow, and he knew how to achieve it. *Make people laugh.* He needed harnessing, and I needed time.

The principal came to me.

"Shawn, Ms. Beverly appealed Mr. Dukes' recommendation for expulsion. How will you feel if I overturn it?"

"I'm okay with it."

"You sure?"

"I'll keep an eye on him."

Ms. Beverly won her appeal, and Jamaal returned with a caveat: He couldn't join the student council. Jamaal returned penitent. I watched to see if it would stick.

The students stuck to their outrage. They civilly petitioned for Jamaal's reenlistment and passed several sheets around the school. We had 2,200 students and 3,000 signatures. Even Mr. Burgess and Ms. Donna Mays signed the petition. Guess who didn't?

Jamaal ran counter-culturally. They vied for his reinstatement, and he vied against it. Several times, he told students, "No, he's my mentor. He told me what to do, but I didn't follow." I could work with that.

"Jamaal, everyone wants you back on the student council."

"Yeah, but I didn't follow your lead."

"It's fine. I'm a grown-up. You're the one I'm concerned with. Do you want to do it?"

"Yeah, of course, but—"

"No announcements."

"No problem."

"Get out of here."

"Got it."

"And, Jamaal . . ."

"Yeah?"

"They need you."

> LEADERS CREATE LEADERSHIP OPPORTUNITIES
> SO FOLLOWERS HAVE SOMEONE TO FOLLOW.

Jamaal needed the student council more than the student council needed him. It gave him direction. Jamaal led people with or without joining an organized body; the student council pointed the way. As his junior and senior years passed, he continued serving without incident, but the clock wound down, and he still lacked direction. I'd seen this film before, and I didn't want it to end as a cliffhanger.

As a high school athlete, I led on the football field but didn't lead my life. I led others before I could lead myself, and that's dangerous. I knew Jamaal needed help and direction after high school, so I intervened.

"You need to get into school."

"What do I gotta do?"

"ACT first."

He scored high enough to attend Claflin University, but he didn't have a way there. I knew what I had to do. I drove Jamaal and his mom to Claflin University, and we met with one of the vice presidents.

The VP introduced himself to Jamaal and Ms. Beverly and wasted no time addressing the obvious.

"Jamaal, we'll admit you despite your defunct grades, but you must prove I made the right decision."

"I will. I promise."

"Don't make promises. Make the grades. Do you know where to get your books?"

"No, sir."

"Do you have money? You didn't file for financial aid," he looked at Ms. Beverly and then back to Jamaal, "and I'm sure you would qualify."

"We didn't file for aid. I'm sorry."

"Don't be sorry. Go get your books."

The VP handed Jamaal his credit card. Jamaal and Ms. Beverly sat silently for a minute, and the VP said, "Go get your books," so Jamaal took off for the bookstore while Ms. Beverly gathered the financial aid paperwork.

Quick Tips

> ➢ When preparation isn't enough, sometimes we provide.
> ➢ You can't make a horse drink, but you can lead it to water.
> ➢ You need the right people; look for them.

The VP had served on my doctoral dissertation committee, and we'd spoken before I brought Jamaal to Claflin. I'd explained I had a student who didn't have the grades but needed an opportunity, and the rest is history.

Jamaal earned a presidential scholarship that year, which paid for his undergraduate degree in mass communications—go figure. As a first-generation college graduate, he broke the family mold. He called me often, seeking advice. At times, Ms. Beverly called, fearing Jamaal would derail, and requesting I help him get back on track. But after we turn around, that doesn't mean we've *turned* around.

Since graduating high school, Jamaal has become a success story. He's been on *Put a Ring on It*, a reality television series that airs on the Oprah Winfrey Network. He's promoted several podcasts and television series, and he made the 40 under 40 list for successful persons who graduated from Claflin University. And as they say in Jamaal's business, "Wait, there's more." Jamaal gives back. He serves. He donates to his college. He's involved in the community. He serves today, so he can lead tomorrow. He's a born/built leader.

Denouement

A standard plot diagram has five points: Exposition, Rising Action, Climax, and Denouement, which is pronounced *day-noo-MAH*. In the denouement, the author ties a pretty bow around the story so the reader's not left wondering too much, but enough to keep them interested if there will be a sequel. Jamaal's the sequel. He's like a son to me.

I had met Jamaal when I was a wet-behind-the-ears, twenty-six-year-old assistant principal. Jamaal was sixteen. We grew into our roles together. I gave him a taste of leadership, and he gave me a taste of leadership pride. For a sophomoric clown to earn scholarships, degrees, awards, and multiple recognitions, they must overcome seemingly insurmountable obstacles. And I got to be part of it. I helped. Just like Coach Young helped me, and I'm sure, just like someone else helped Coach Young. Whom do you help?

Leaders create leaders. That's the goal. Service was the journey. Coach Young served me by talking to Coach Abrams, taking me to college, and helping me with the scholarship paperwork. I served Jamaal by giving him a taste of leadership, talking to the VP, and taking him to college. We helped make a way.

Discernment Decisions

Shawn Foster

> Did we overserve by driving young men to a college not too far away? Should we have left them to "figure it out" before they even got there? Should I have asked Jamaal's mom to appeal my decision? Should he have been allowed on the student council after his debacle?

Discernment decisions loom large. *We don't have all the right answers, but we do have the right to seek some.* I've made plenty of bad decisions, and like Jamaal, when I have, I've fessed up. As a leader, *we must confess our failures, and we must pin up our accomplishments.* We do both.

I'm very proud of my experiences with Jamaal. He's created some of my proudest moments in educational leadership. That's not pride talking; it's s an experience I'm proud of. It takes a village to make that happen, and it took service in perpetuity for us to get there.

Pride, on the other hand, is much more insidious. People often say, "Pride goes before the fall," but the actual quote is, "Pride goes before destruction, and a haughty spirit before a fall."[10] *Pride will destroy a leader's ability to discern, and contempt will make a leader fall.* Pride makes statements like, "If I did it for one, I can do it for all!"

Losing Time

My career trajectory careened up and to the right. On a graph, that's good, what we like to see. After I finished my second master's degree, a colleague, Dr. Lavern Byrd, pushed me to pursue a doctorate. Actually, she pulled. I didn't want it. She said, "You need it to become a principal." I sighed. She took me with her. She registered me for the Miller's Analogies Test (MAT) and came knocking before sunrise one Saturday.

"Yes, Dr. Byrd. It's *early*."

"I said you're coming with me."

"Yes, Dr. Byrd."

I passed the test and enrolled in a doctoral program. Dr. Byrd dragged me through all that, then took an assistant principal position at another school. She should have been ashamed of herself—ruining my Saturday mornings. I continued as assistant director; then, I got promoted to Dorman High School, where I met Jamaal. But I never forgot Dr. Byrd. A few years later, I got promoted again to principal at Fairforest Middle School. I took *her* with me to serve as one of two assistant principals.

I had one and needed one. I interviewed a huge teddy bear of a man named Brian Linder. He walked through the doorway and blocked the light. He ducked underneath the exit signs. He made college football players look *small*. When Brian moved like a man on a mission, everybody stepped aside. Everybody.

I completed my doctorate and received another promotion. But in Spartanburg, we had a problem school whose reputation preceded it. Poorly. The name Whitlock Junior High School made people shudder.

Shawn Foster

Most avoided it for good reasons: crime, danger, violence, smelly teenagers with attitudes. As I wrote, I got promoted.

The superintendent called me.

"Shawn, we have a position for you."

"What's that?"

"We have a new model we're instituting, and we need someone to oversee it. We want to make Whitlock a Turnaround school, and we think you're the man for the job."

"Is this a promotion or a demotion?"

"Whatever you choose it to be."

"Let me have a few days to think."

I did a lot of thinking. I didn't want to dive into shallow water, and I'd need a *team*. I fought the battle of competing goods. I had a great job and a great team, but I also had a great opportunity. The battle of competing goods pits two good options against each other and drives an anxiety wedge into our hearts when we overthink them. *What should I do? Should I stay or should I go?* It's like having two dates for Saturday and stressing over the choice when we could be date*less*, cleaning our fingernails.

Should I leave Fairforest? If I stay, I'll—Wham! I collided with a student at the interchange between outside and inside. He stared at me, trembling.

"Young man, what are you doing?"

"I wasn't doing nothing."

"I can see that."

He looked vaguely familiar, which sent off alarm bells. I *prided* myself on knowing every student's name. Why didn't I know his?

"Why are you standing outside? Do you go to school here?"

"I just transferred."

"From?"

"Whitlock."

"Again, what are you doing?"

"I'm not doing anything. I transferred from Whitlock, and nobody will give me a chance."

I understood his sentiment, and I understood my answer. I returned to the office, pondering how to build a team that could handle Whitlock.

Knee Deep

It was 100 percent African American, 100 percent poverty-stricken, and 100 percent my new responsibility. When I told the team my decision, Brian said, "I'm coming with you." I sighed.

Did I mention Brian was White? Did I mention he also wrestled professionally under the name PrimeTime Brian Linder? What type of sigh do you think I sighed?

"All right, Brian. Why?"

"Shawn, I went to Whitlock."

"Is that where you got your fashion sense?"

I required my male assistant principals to wear shirts, ties, and suit jackets daily. Brian wore the same jacket no matter what. Purple shirt, olive green jacket, no problem. Red shirt, blue pants, olive green jacket, even better. I'd politely mentioned this, "Man, you've *got* to upgrade your wardrobe game! You're killing me," but he said, "You said a coat and tie. You didn't say they had to match."

He wasn't wrong.

I'd disrupted his train of thought with my clothing quip, and he looked hurt.

"You don't believe me, do you?"

"I haven't known you to lie, Brian. But Whitlock is all Black."

"Shawn, I was the only White kid. Listen, I know how it feels not to fit in, not to get noticed, to be a void, like those kids do. When I attended Whitlock, not only was I the only White kid, but I was a big, gangly son of a gun. When I got noticed, I got beat.

"One day, several kids chased me for a beatdown, and I barely had the lead on them. I burst into the gym, betting they wouldn't follow me. They didn't, but I made so much noise everything stopped. The coach took one look at my oversized body and said, 'You here for basketball tryouts?' And I said yes, just to save my skin. That's how I stumbled into sports. If it hadn't been for that day, I'd have spent the rest of my life running. I understand their lives, Shawn, and I can help."

Then I understood why he looked hurt; he saw his chances to help were fleeting if I didn't believe he attended Whitlock. I found it doubtful anyone overlooked the one White kid at Whitlock, especially one who shaved in seventh grade, but that was Brian's experience. Leaders don't argue about experiences; we assign directions. I made two decisions.

Shawn Foster

One, I would go to the superintendent and confirm I'd take the job if I could take Brian with me, and two, *regardless of people's exteriors, we don't know their experiences.*

- Brian was White; the students were Black.
- Brian felt undervalued; the students felt undervalued.
- Brian had struggles; the students had struggles.
- Brian had passions; the students had passions.
- Brian didn't fit the exterior mold, but he shared the same scars.

I took Brian with me. I also swindled Lisa Dawson and Sharell McDowell, two of the finest English teachers on God's green earth, to come, too, since I'm an opportunist. It went something like this.

"I'm going to Whitlock."

"If you're going to Whitlock, I'm going to Whitlock."

"Yeah, me too."

"Done."

I took them all with me: one African American female, a White female, and a White former top-rope jumping, Eiffel Tower knocking, 290-lb assistant principal. I had my team. And I had my dream: *We do it for one; we do it for all.*

Losing Time 2.0

We sweated it out through another sticky South Carolina summer. Summers here smolder, but "it ain't the heat that'll kill you." It's the rain! In the South, people complain about humidity, as if having a dewy morning driveway competes with a lake of fire. We top one another's stories with anecdotes about our "car" dress shirt since we stained the other while walking from the house. But I rarely hear anyone mention the rain. In Spartanburg, we average two to five inches per summer month. Seattle averages less than two. We just don't advertise it while we drink our sweet tea.

Brian and I worked through the summer, dodging thunderstorms within and without. When leading a new school, you must *throw* yourself into the community. We had to. Leaders can't build a community without the community. We needed them, and they needed us. And I wanted everyone to belong.

Leaders often raise symbolic flags to equity and inclusion, but I focus on belonging instead. If everyone's included, individuals reside but don't belong. When community members belong to a group, it's theirs, and they take pride in it. I'm included in the over-forty club, but that doesn't mean I want to be. However, I belong to Tanya—just ask her; she'll tell you—and that's exactly what I want. *To be strong, we must belong.*

Since we couldn't occupy two spaces at once, Brian focused on internal operations first, then on external connections, and I focused on community engagement first, then on internal operations. Luckily, August 2009 was extremely dry, but I still had sweat rings when I went outdoors. We were tag-team champions, and he came through in the clutch. He built a community with staff who didn't look, speak, or act like him. They felt *appreciated*. I guess he read Dale Carnegie, too.

Brian's passion imbued new and returning teachers; I considered it a good omen. After our sweaty summer, we stood proudly on the first day of school: the stalls and walls scrubbed, the processes defined, our attitudes refined—and day one went off with a *BANG!* Students received class schedules, arrived at classes early, engaged, and followed the processes. The returning teachers gloated pridefully, which spoke volumes.

Progress Update

We've transitioned into a new season. Now, we are experiencing new leadership and old hats. Leaders who expect no disturbances while enacting new processes haven't evaluated leadership deeply. New seasons bring new realizations, not only for us but also for those we lead. *People fear the unfamiliar.* Watch how this unfolds as we transition into more unfamiliar situations.

We had a candy-coated first week. The students loved Brian! He was good for them. Lisa and Sharell reported similar successes. By Friday, I smiled ear to ear. We worked the weekend. Often, during a start-up, we pulled seven-day work weeks, and week one required it. On Sunday, Brian left the campus before me, and we shared a knowing nod as he walked out. We had done well.

The next thing I knew, someone said, "Brian's been killed in a car accident."

Tragedy Strikes

Tragedy rips through lives, disregarding human considerations. A celebrity's plane crashes; a son falls to a drive-by. An infant dies from SIDS the same day a grandfather drives into a tree. Cancer steals one, and cocaine steals another. Tragedy is an insatiable fiend who never says, "Enough!"

Knee Deep

With a guy like Brian, you can't get enough. He made us laugh, coming and going. He'd walk through a stifled room and drop an off-center one-liner that'd leave us in stitches, and if we heard laughter in the halls, we'd find Brian at the center. The staff at Whitlock only had a few weeks with him, but I felt the loss personally. He was my friend.

After his funeral, we still had a school to run, and his memory took us with him, pulling us forward into rooms with kids who needed us. In instances like these, one often asks, "Why do good people die?" My best answer is so we can appreciate what they did when they were alive.

Brian built relationships. We continued to build relationships. Brian made us laugh. We continued to create laughter. Brian brought his passion. We brought ours. We appreciated him more when we only had his memory.

When Brian died, I lost a friend and a dream. I only needed to lose one. I lost the dream that *if I did it for one, I can do it for all!* I had busted my butt working with Brian, but tragedy stole him away. He didn't deserve to die; it just happened. I couldn't save him any more than I could save you. I've worked with thousands of students. I couldn't save them all. I learned a terribly hard lesson from a terribly difficult tragedy. *We do for all in hopes that we can save some.* We do the work, but we don't control the outcome.

Inevitably, as leaders, we'll polish our success trophy, name it Jamaal, and then believe we can duplicate it for all. But that's a fool's errand. We overdo it. As I wrote, you can fill a gallon jug with only so much water. The rest spills over and supersedes our capacity to clean it up. But we want more, and *when* we get it, we're screwed. Instead of being grateful for what we have, we set the expectations that destroy us. *Discerning leaders know when to say "when."*

That week, I lost Superman's touch and Vanity's pinch. What we do matters, but it doesn't matter most. We're not God. I couldn't save everybody; I couldn't even save my friend.

My friend Brian passed away at 35; he was survived by his parents, stepparents, brother, grandmother, and a grateful memory. Every sweat I broke that year reminded me of Brian, and every olive-green suit jacket still does. *Good leaders leave us wanting more.*

Shawn Foster

Pole Position

As a child, I played the Formula One-inspired arcade game *Pole Position*. Drivers hugged corners and then slingshot straightaways while sweaty-armed teenagers crouched over the controls. The fastest time earned the pole, and everyone wanted to be first. While the rubber melted the road, the drivers pressed forward. No cars inched near their tail, anxiety-pressing them, nor clipped their wing, sending them spinning. In the time trial, drivers drove alone.

I relearned that lesson in my first half of college football when I glanced into Mom-less stands and had to stand alone. No family member propelled me, compelled me, or impelled me; I had to self-will myself. That wasn't the race; that was the "for the time being" trial.

After earning a pole in *Pole Position*, drivers skidded through corners and rocketed straightaways, seeking a checkered flag. The true race had begun. Competition. Unfriendly competition. The kind of competition where followers discouraged you, hoping you'd crash into gasoline-licking flames as they sped past, laughing. Suddenly, a gentle leader snuck out front, and drivers zeroed in, gunning for her position. Then came the rush. Adrenaline peaked in her ears as noses inched near her tail. She felt exposed. It's vulnerable out front.

Leaders lead from various positions: in the boardroom, in the break room, behind closed doors, from the podium, behind the curtain, beneath the wreckage, from the sideline, and beside the opposition, but invariably, *leaders must lead from the front*. And it's not the front if nobody guns for you.

After Brian passed, I learned leaders build succession plans and crisis plans. Leaders who don't act until a crisis occurs are two steps behind. Three cultures exist: a culture of urgency, a culture of complacency, and a culture of crisis. We must focus while in a culture of urgency—as the norm. If we function in a culture of complacency, we'll find ourselves in a culture of crisis—more to come in subsequent chapters. The action must predate the tragedy.

Leaders prepare for the worst and . . . the best. You thought I would say, "And hope for the best," didn't you? We do both. We lead through successes and failures since both are inevitable.

I prepared for the inevitabilities, understanding I couldn't predict all the eventualities. As the principal at Spartanburg High School Freshman Academy, I never enacted our major crisis plan due to tragedy, but I pushed my succession plan. I pushed vigorously, and my assistant principals constantly checked their rearview mirrors. I had a record to keep: Every assistant principal who sought a principal's position under my mentorship achieved it. A 100-percent success rate. I knew what it took. *A friendly shove in the back is better than failure's slap in the face.*

Face the Problem; Earn the Pole

Nicole Thompson had a problem. I was her boss. She had another problem. She was *her* boss. And the *her* who Nicole led, hated *her.* Confused? We've all had a *her* or *him*—persons we deigned to call by name because they're so undignified in our mind. We relegate them to personal pronouns: "I can't freaking stand *her.*" In Nicole's scenario, she played the undignified monster in a specific teacher's fears, and that specific teacher haunted Nicole's nightmares: They were each other's *her.*

Nicole worked tirelessly. She displayed punctuality, preparedness, precision, and personality but lacked one important *P*. I admired her tenacity as a disciplined African American female assistant principal. I knew what it took. I saw her unlimited potential, but I owed her more. She brought me her problem, but I gave her a push.

"Dr. Foster, Ms. Complainsalot manufactures lies and spreads them like chicken feed. I can't stand *her*! *She* underperforms, then makes excuses during our coaching sessions. THEN, she turns it on me: running around telling people I'm targeting *her.*"

Shawn Foster

I'm so lucky. Teachable moments fall in my lap like cookie crumbs. I'd been waiting for this one, nearly praying for it. I'd coached Nicole repeatedly outside the fire. I'd shoot her one-liners like, "You need to recognize their emotions without being emotional," or, "It's okay to be friendly and not be friends," but my maxims often ruffled her feathers. This time, I could finally coach her through the fire. Do you think I stopped my one-liners?

She railed on. "She says I harass *her*. Like I have time to harass *her*! I feel like I'm wasting my time."

Time Out

If you're in leadership, this is worth writing on a sticky note and adhering to your computer monitor, phone, or mirror. When people target leaders, they also follow a process. *Objectors create a narrative.*

I'm using the very personal pronoun *you* here to offend you. When people target leaders, that's the goal: to make *you* play defense.

Narrative Intimidation Process

1. *You* are not committed; *you* are not one of us.
2. *You* are not trustworthy; *you* are a cheater or liar.
3. *You* don't have the money, power, or pull to do what *you* say.
4. *You* are going to get fired!

Each statement undermines your credibility. You're not invested; you don't belong—you'll abandon *us*. You've stolen your position. You practice infidelity. You have another boyfriend or girlfriend, or you've slept your way into leadership—you're incompetent and untrustworthy. You make empty promises, and if you keep them, you keep them through nefarious means. And, finally, if all else fails, *we'll* take your job, your livelihood, your family, and if it gets severe enough, your life.

That's what you are up against: next-level life-altering attacks. However, when you recognize this pattern—when you read your sticky note—it creates freedom. You realize it's not about you. It's about . . .

Time In

There are appropriate times to work alongside one another, but when coaching leaders, sometimes we must tailgate them. Nicole's tone told me what time it was. I did what all good leaders do. I scratched my cheek. Then, I grinned, and she dang near came unhinged.

"Why are you smiling, Dr. Foster? This isn't funny!"

I launched into one of my famous monologues, throwing gasoline on the fire.

> When will you allow people to be who they are? The minute you are okay with people being who they are . . . You know what? You think too much of yourself. Do you think people wake up every day thinking so much of you that they expand their feelings and emotions because Nicole is so important? People don't hold you in that high of regard. You are just standing there—you are in the way. You are the person who is in her way, so you become the target. Once you can look beyond what you think about yourself, you can help. Until then, you can't help anybody. Come to think of it, you're standing in your own way. When people lash out—when they make up things—that's who they are. That's how they deal with conflict and their stress, Nicole. How do you deal with yours?

She contorted in her chair and eyeballed the ceiling, all while clenching her jaw. I understood her feelings, believing I'd turned on her like I was one of *them*. Good. *Leaders practice in innocuous settings so they can play when a crisis comes.* This was target practice.

At that moment, Gavin Fisher knocked, and I waved him in. Gavin kept his nose to the grindstone and served as Nicole's counterpart. They made a great racing team and often drafted from each other. They were a one-two punch, and as I figured, he tried to come to her aid.

"She's not wrong, Dr. Foster. Ms. Complainsalot is an expert at character assassination."

"See, Gavin gets it too. It's not just *me!*"

"Nicole, you can't use him to validate your feelings. He shares the same shortcomings as you."

Talk about an answered prayer: I got a two-for-one sale!

They departed the office with quiet mouths and loud eyes while I leaned back in my chair. I'm sure Nicole's heels nearly punctured the stairs, climbing to the second floor. I let them sit in the driver's seat, feeling the rush, looking around for who'd gun them down next.

Quick Tips

> - Leaders test character.
> - Leaders offend to see if followers take it or overcome it.
> - Leaders seek solutions, not validations.

That afternoon, I wedged beside their office and heard, "We stay late, we do everything *he* asks, and this is how we get treated! I'm not working Saturdays or Sundays anymore. I'm not staying late anymore, either. *He* can do it his damn self."

I opened the door. "Guys, time for duty." I closed the door.

The following morning, on Saturday, I drove through the near-empty parking lot and parked beside Gavin and Nicole. When I opened their office door, Nicole said, "Don't say anything!" and we laughed it off together. They got it. The *P* that Nicole lacked and Gavin needed to gain wasn't push. They had that. They desperately needed perseverance: ongoing strength under duress. The key wasn't to become stronger; the key was to become self-assured. To think: *What they think of me is none of my business—it's theirs.*

When we're out front, we're vulnerable; everybody guns for us. When we recognize the game, we expect it, and we don't fear the pole position; we switch to a bird's-eye view.

Nicole Thompson became the principal of Carver Middle School in Spartanburg School District 7. Gavin Fisher became the principal of John E. Ewing Middle School in Cherokee County School District 1. I kept my perfect principal-placing streak and eventually had to take my own medicine. Not yet, but soon, very soon.

Knee Deep

> **Progress Update**
>
> We're near the halfway point, not quite, but almost. The best leaders know when to remove themselves. We can't see how great the party is from the dance floor; sometimes, we must enjoy it from the balcony. During Nicole's leadership commencement ball, Ms. Complainsalot was her dance partner. They did not enjoy their time. However, when Nicole ditched her ego and stepped back, she could finally see *her* as someone who just wanted to dance alone.

Shawn Foster

Bet on Yourself

We downed chicken wings and drank beer. I monitored his stingy fingers, but Cyrus pointed at the sports highlight overhead, and while a young man self-suspended over a basketball rim, Cyrus stole two chicken wings before the sauce could run.

"You're lucky you're my fraternity brother."

"Or what?"

"Now, you're lucky you're my best friend, Cyrus."

"Or what? What would you do in Buffalo Wild Wings surrounded by all these people?"

"Call Tanya."

"Call your wife! Ha! What kind of man are you? Will you say, 'Honey, Cyrus is being mean again; he stole my chicken wings'? I dare you—"

"She'll call Phoebe."

Cyrus scraped three wings onto my plate. As one of the wisest leaders I've ever met, Cyrus knew *when* he was whipped.

"That's what I thought, brother Cyrus, that's what I thought."

We grubbed through hot wings and sipped our beers, and my mind wandered to far-off places where life-changing decisions collide with self-doubting dreams.

"A penny for your thoughts."

"Man, they ain't gonna hire me."

"Why do you say that?"

"I've never been to Aiken before."

"So?"

"Look at the numbers. That's the sixth-largest school district in South Carolina. Twenty-six thousand students, forty-two schools. We have seven."

"Seven what?"

"Seven thousand students. And it's too conservative over there. They won't hire an African American man to be deputy superintendent, especially one without superintendent experience."

"So, they won't hire you because you're Black? Or because you're inexperienced?"

"The county is too red."

"Man, I don't know anybody who knows more about education than you or could make a bigger impact. Let's say you get the job, and—"

"And they fire me."

"At least you can say you did the job. If you get fired, you're back to being a director. Imagine that. Your fallback job is better than most people's dream job. How many people are dying for the chance to be a director? Your failure plan is better than their success plan."

I tried my psychology on him. "What I hear you saying is—"

"What you hear me saying is, 'Let's make a bet.'"

He never took his eyes off me. He looked me dead in the eyes and pulled a dollar from his wallet, slapping it on the table.

"I'll bet on you to get the job. You bet against yourself that you won't."

We shook greasy hands across the table.

Take the Bet

Leaders need leaders. Coaches need coaches. High performers need high performers. We all need community, accountability, someone holding us up lest we fall, and someone to help us when we do. When you find yourself standing alone, that's good—that's leadership. But when you find yourself without companionship, that's isolation. *Endless isolation is imprisonment.*

Cyrus manipulated me, and I took the bait. See, good leaders manipulate. Imagine teaching an infant to walk. She's pulled herself up, her longing eyes beckoning you to hold her. You coo, shaking her favorite toy, standing so close, only a few stumbles away, calling her out. She reaches, leans, and stumbles forward two steps, and then you snag her high, praising her efforts. You manipulated her, but not to *your* advantage. Maybe it's to your detriment, for in a few weeks, you'll be chasing her with a spoonful of mushed peas. You manipulated her for her good.

Cyrus knew what I wanted, just like you knew what the baby wanted. It's no different than adding fertilizer to the soil. However, when we add fertilizer, but afterward cut people at the root and parade around stealing their credit, saying, "I did that! I did that," we fail them and ourselves. We cast a wicked spell for our benefit.

Cyrus didn't do that. He baited me, and I took the bait and the bet. Using reverse psychology, Cyrus flipped me from doubting to acting. I applied for the job despite my fears. Cyrus was right. The worst thing I imagined wasn't too bad at all. I had a good job, and the worst I'd get from Aiken was a rejection. It didn't happen.

A few weekends later, Cyrus and I celebrated again and got a little too rowdy, and he called Phoebe, begging permission to crash at my place. She granted it. Whew! Understand, Cyrus always over-partied; he went out of his way to celebrate his friends. When he drove through the South Carolina countryside, he'd call up a friend in the next town and say, "I'm coming by. I just want to lay eyes on you." He'd meet them for lunch, grab a drink, or whatever made them feel celebrated. That Friday, we over-celebrated my upcoming interview. Everyone laughed it off the morning after, and while Cyrus prepared to take his son back to college, I prepared for my Monday morning interview in Aiken.

On April 13, at 4:00 a.m., my phone buzzed, and I whisked it from the nightstand.

"Hello?"

"Shawn, sorry to bother you, man. I know it's early, but did you hear about Cyrus?"

"Hear what?"

"He's gone. Cyrus is deceased."

"I don't believe it. He just spent the night in the guest room. I'll call Phoebe and call you back."

"Okay."

"Hey, Phoebe, I know it's early. How are you doing?"

She burst into tears. She never said anything, but I knew my nightmare was true. I called my friend back quickly, sitting straight up in the bed. When I finished the call, I turned to Tanya. "I'm not going. Cyrus was my best friend. I can't do this interview now. We need to be there for his family."

Tanya slowly turned her eyes, looking at me the way Tanya does, and said, "Is that what Cyrus would want you to do?"

The drive to Aiken didn't improve matters. There I sat, driving on Cyrus's dollar. I had lots of questions and very few answers. When I walked in, despite my smile and formal attire, I'm sure my eyes told another story.

"Thank you for coming out, Dr. Foster. How are you today?"

"I'm here. I'll do my very best, but I just confirmed that my best friend died last night."

They shared their condolences and conducted the interview, and everything went fine, though my mind traveled to far-off places where chicken bones meet burial plots, and we can't believe our friends are gone.

The day after Cyrus's funeral, I had a second interview. Again, they shared their condolences, and again, the interview went fine. Again, my mind traveled off to far-off places where we share greasy handshakes and laughter with ghosts.

A week later, I got a call from Aiken. They offered me the job, and I accepted it. I turned to Cyrus's memory and said, "I owe you a dollar, buddy. I wish I could have given it to you."

Shawn Foster

Taken

I'd taken the bet, and I would live with the consequences. The consequences of being appointed the deputy superintendent in a large county like Aiken meant the community dumped truckloads of responsibilities in my lap, and as the first African American to hold that position, many of those responsibilities were unrelated to education. Some were related to being first.

Before I could thank God for the opportunity, my phone buzzed.

"Congratulations, Shawn. Hey, when you get some time, do you think you could—"

"Hey, brother. Good job. I've got this opportunity to—"

"Now that you have that position in Aiken, how about we—"

I'd prioritized service, and people shimmied from behind the woodwork, holding their hands out. Before I could blink, I got another call. "Brother Foster, we're very proud of your accomplishment, and we'd be honored to have you as Saturday's Achievement Week guest speaker."

It was Tuesday.

"We had a guest speaker prepared for Omega Psi Phi, but unfortunately, Cyrus Hinton recently passed away. Did you know him?"

Did I know him? "He was my best friend. I'd be honored. I'll be there Saturday."

As the district counselor for District 6—the elected attorney—Cyrus had programs to attend and questions to answer, and since we gave scholarships during Achievement Week, he had award ceremony speeches to give. That was his job. The speeches became mine.

My best friend is gone, and they want me to replace him? I can't replace him, but he bet me that dollar, so I will make it count. This isn't a coincidence; this is a continuation. Then I remembered his voice, "How many people are dying for the chance—?"

When You're Gone

Building a legacy is a farce. We can't control how we're remembered because we can't control others' memories. Today's venerated saints become tomorrow's scandal story. It's a matter of others' perspective, not ours.

Let's focus on what we can do while we're still living. Can you look yourself in the eye, read your obituary, and know it's true? If not, then you must initiate change. But it must be a balanced change. Don't throw out the good with the bad. Use the good to change the bad. But how will you know the good if you can't see it in yourself? That requires perspective, and one way to obtain that perspective is by spotting the good in others.

It works both ways. Just like you can see others' failures and then spot your own, you can also see good in others and yourself. And when you see what's good, you become grateful. Gratitude changes your perspective from "I don't have enough" to "I'm grateful for." Gratitude changes your statements from "I wish I still had . . ." to "I'm thankful I had the opportunity to . . ." This idea was so powerful that I placed a sign outside my office door: "Start every day with grace and gratitude." It reminds me when I walk in.

I'm grateful to honor Cyrus's memory, and I'd dishonor him if I wallowed in his loss. He bet a dollar on me that I would fight harder with the odds stacked against me and not give up when the road got tough. When Cyrus died, the road got tough, but his faith in me gave me eyes to see my way forward. His actions mattered to *me.*

That being said, I've written an obituary for Cyrus. Remember, the deceased don't hear their obituaries; obituaries comfort those left behind.

Shawn Foster

Cyrus

O'Shun Cyrus Hinton of Spartanburg, South Carolina, died April 12, 2015, but fully lived all forty-seven of his years. He dearly loved his wife, Phoebe, during their twenty-four-year marriage, and, knowing Cyrus, he carried her with him in his heart. He gave himself to his sons, pouring every last drop into his family.

Some men are too great for this world and pursue right so fervently they upset all that is wrong. Cyrus was one of those men. He magnified the unseen so we could see the truth. He advocated for truth. He told the truth. He protected the truth. He revealed what we know to be true but were too afraid to grasp. We know he lived his life fully, for when we observed Cyrus, we saw what we wanted to be.

Cyrus was the wisest man I ever met. He never faltered over what he didn't understand; he focused on his beliefs. He investigated, he challenged, he invested, he gave, he loved, and he believed that tomorrow would hold more than today foretold. Cyrus believed abundance lies around every corner if only we will seek it. In seeking it, Cyrus added life to my life and all of ours. He added in his life, and he added in his death. Cyrus gave us something to believe, and we appreciate it more now that he's left it with us. And what did he leave with us? Cyrus gave us a gamble of truth, a slice of life, and an ingredient of hope. Cyrus taught us:

> **Don't Fear Failure; Bet on Success**
> When you face an opportunity, seek it, believing you can reach it. If you don't fully give yourself over to your dream, you'll fail when adversity strikes. Adversity will strike, so bet on yourself before it does.
>
> **Count the Cost, Not the Loss**
> All encounters, endeavors, and experiences require risk. Too often, we count potential loss instead of potential costs. For every gain, there will be a loss, but without sowing, we cannot

reap. Those who only count loss will lose what they have, for all we have returns to dust.

From the Bitter Comes the Sweet
When we bake a cake, we add bitter eggs, without which the cake would fall to pieces. We need all the ingredients, not just the sugar. Without adversity in life, we never enjoy its sweetness. We think more sweetness will make it sweeter but forget that too much sweetness makes us sick.

Cyrus taught me one final thing: Consequences are returns on investments; they're not all bad. Being Cyrus's friend saddled me with consequences, and I'd take a double dose because, consequently, everything he taught me was *good.**

---

*When I wrote the final sentence of Cyrus's obituary, I repeatedly mistyped "good" as "food." Maybe Cyrus was telling me something. Cheers, buddy!

Shawn Foster

Teachable Moments

Rain sheets pelted our windshield, drowning our vision in halos. A red light flashed; an eighteen-wheeler drifted into our lane, narrowly missing our front bumper. I lay on the horn, holding it down for charismatic emphasis. He got the picture. I swerved right and rode the rumble strips: a tree branch in the road, excitement in the car.

When I drive with Tanya, our rides are always exciting. We have multiple opportunities for candid conversations that bridge relational differences: I drive, and she provides commentary on my driving. On this particular drive, our joyful experience extended over 108 miles from Spartanburg to Aiken. Did I mention the rain?

After Aiken County Public Schools hired me, not only did I receive opportunities to serve in various external capacities, but I also got to do some educational work, too. I'd been hired as the deputy superintendent, so I had to push away some of the outside requests and focus on being the deputy superintendent. My first task included driving to Aiken, attending a board meeting, and conducting a meet-and-greet between my family and the meeting attendees. Simple enough, except this action required me to drive over one hundred miles in a torrential downpour, all while Tanya instructed me how to navigate through the buckets of rain. Her instructions were not suggestions.

We strapped Alyx and Aden in their car seats. As we pulled from the driveway into a light mist, the kids didn't care much for our evening-time country drive, but we support one another's endeavors in our family, and we instituted this practice early, so they acquiesced. Soon, the six-year-old and two-year-old fell asleep in the back seat, but the fussing started up front.

Knee Deep

Mile 1. "Shawn, you're driving too close to that van. Get off their bumper."

Mile 3. "Shawn, you should speed up and follow more closely. In this rain, you'll see better with that vehicle blocking some of it."

Mile 7. "Shawn, do you see how hard it's raining? You need to be careful. This weather is awful. The clouds are making it too dark."

Fortunately, the increasing downpour created more opportunities for Tanya to help me improve my driving. I always say, "If you can't take criticism, you can't expect to grow," and Tanya made sure I drove on the growth track. We'll call it the Highway to Heaven.

As the rain increased, my responses decreased, not to the dangers outside the vehicle but to the distractions within it. Tanya noticed. Since I hadn't adhered to her advice, she tried another tactic. She increased the volume, suspecting the rain had dulled my hearing.

Mile 37. "Pull over! Put on your hazards! These cars can't see you. Why aren't you responding? Did you put on your flashers?!"

I continued driving peacefully, hands at ten and two, eyes ahead, aiming high while steering. Unfortunately, I couldn't see more than two feet past the hood, so I aimed at hitting nothing. Then, I caught something from the corner of my eye. Smoke! For a moment, I thought our engine had overheated, but I soon realized the smoke rolled from Tanya's ears.

Mile 46. "So, you're ignoring me now? You have our babies in here, driving through a hurricane, and you're not going to respond to me?"

I hit the rumble strips.

"Shawn! Pay attention to the road!"

I passed a sidelined car.

"Shawn! You can't pass people in this downpour. Are you crazy?"

I must be.

The rainwater slowly washed away from the tires as I cautiously drove between the lines. Ahead, a smattering of brake lights collected beneath a well-lit overpass, and Tanya spotlighted the opportunity.

Mile 54. "Shawn, see that bridge right there! Pull over under that bridge! Are you ignoring me? You don't turn on your hazards! You don't pull over! You don't do anything I . . . what the—"

When I straddled two lanes after passing under the underpass, Tanya used choice words. She selected four-letter words, but not the ones like *love*, *care*, *hope*, or *babe*. She didn't realize that I couldn't pull over without hitting the parked cars, and then the eighteen-wheeler swerved into our lane. After I heralded him with the horn, Tanya used more choice words about my decision-making and how I risked our children's lives.

Mile 82. "Finally, the rain is slowing down." The rain decreased to a pitter-patter, but my heart rose into my throat. We only had twenty more minutes of driving left, and Tanya smoldered next to me, so I needed to defuse the situation. Now, I don't watch many movies, but I've seen *The Negotiator* and how Samuel L. Jackson negotiated his way out of a very hairy situation. I channeled his skills.

I remained silent. Tanya terminated her one-sided conversation with me and turned her attention to the kids. She discussed their feelings and ensured they felt safe while redlining beside me. If Tanya were the car engine, she would have overheated long ago. I had to convince her to pull over in her mind and let the engine cool. And then Samuel L. spoke to me: "Tell her how driving through the storm worked for her benefit."

Brilliant!

"Tanya, I want to talk to you."

"Oh? You want to talk to me now?"

"I want to explain something; this is the best lesson we could have."

"You're always speaking in parables."

"You know those people who pulled over? They feel safer, but they're not. Sure, they're not getting rained on, but they're still in the heart of the storm while we're on the other side. See, we had a destination in mind. Sometimes, we have to blow the horn, drive down the middle, or slow down, but the moment we stop, we're stuck in the storm. Things are not always as they appear."

Progress Update

This concludes Part One of the book. We're halfway through the book but only inches from my death. We discussed communication, leadership, quitting, winning, losing, showing up, sticking around, overcoming, serving, leading from the front, facing adversity and tragedy, betting on ourselves, and dying. In Part Two, we'll discuss standing firm in the eye of the storm, especially when we see it coming.

Shawn Foster

Part Two: The Two-Way Mirror

Teachable Moments 2.0

The storm blew over, but another one brewed inside. I thought we'd escaped; we appeared safe, but Tanya had other things on her mind. I settled in for the last few miles, and I think I heard Tanya mention something about "mansplaining" or "things definitely not being as they appear" when she glanced at me sideways.

Mile 103. "Sweetie, could you ever have imagined that this little Black boy from the projects in North Carolina would earn a bachelor's, two master's, and a doctoral degree, all by the age of twenty-eight? I'm going to be the first African American deputy superintendent in Aiken County. In your wildest dreams, could you ever have imagined it?"

Mile 104. Silence.

Mile 105. Silence.

Mile 106. Silence. I started to sweat.

Mile 107. *She's still not speaking to me. I'm getting pissed. I drove us through this storm, got us here safely, and it's still not enough for her. Now we've got to meet all these people, and it'll look like we aren't even speaking. I guess my plan backfired.*

Mile 108. I slowly pulled into the parking lot, coming to a complete stop. Before I shifted into park, Tanya got my attention. She looked me dead in the eyes. "Shawn, I don't know if you've ever been part of my wildest dreams."

Teachable Moment

Just when you think you've arrived, somebody will bring you back to reality. Tanya did that for me, literally and metaphorically. When I felt overconfident, she dashed my hopes against the stones, but, more importantly, she made me laugh. That laughter proved paramount for both of us. We felt free to attend the board meeting with our disagreements behind us, drowning in the storm.

Speaking of storms, when they come, we don't know if we'll weather them, but we must believe we can. If we've put in the preparation, we must lean into our confidence because the outcome is out of our control. The same is true in leadership. When we begin a new initiative, we can't guarantee it will work, but we must maintain faith that it will. We lean into our confidence that the initiative will work or that we'll engineer a better way as we proceed forward. We believe, but we don't guarantee.

Making vows is foolish because we can't guarantee the outcomes of our actions, but lacking vision is also foolish because we can guarantee the outcome of inaction. Things fall apart. When given the opportunity to act, we walk by faith, not by sight. The sight comes later.

That's a keystone habit, a pillar of leadership, the belief that while we're working and nothing seems to change, we will maintain confidence that what we cannot see is changing. When we water a tree, the roots grow whether we see them or not. As leaders, we must remain stable throughout storms, especially when nothing appears to improve.

For many of us, this steadfast leadership concept requires us to change. That's a paradox: Remaining steadfast requires change. We've accustomed ourselves to running around frantically, making changes to create the perception of change; when in reality, we're repeating the same actions and expecting different results. To initiate change, we must change our natural thinking.

When I pursued my master's in counseling, I had a professor shake up this profound idea for me. During a lecture, he asked, "What is the natural thesis of a bird?"

I responded, "To fly."

"To fly where?"

"To fly up."

I thought he'd lost his marbles. *What the hell is this man talking about? Of course, birds fly up. That's how they get to the sky.*

"Have you ever seen a bird in a building? They're trapped. They fly up and around in circles, beating their heads against the ceiling. Even if you open the window, they don't fly out immediately because that requires the bird to do something against its natural thesis. It requires the bird to fly *down*."

Incremental change takes time, and if we can't get comfortable with that idea as leaders, we'll be anxiety-filled pretenders. That's not leadership; that's subversion—it undermines trust. No, when we initiate change, we plug away, plug away, and plug away, and continue to take decisive action. We admit our faults and shortcomings, and we don't cover up. And, we believe. We believe that the world around us changes, even when we don't see it.

That brings me back to the car ride with Tanya. We drove through a storm, and everything changed around us, but we made it out safely. The most profound changes occurred within us. We experienced stress, anxiety, fear, concern, despair, then relief, laughter, joy, and love. On one side of the mirror, we saw the storm around us; on the other side of the mirror, we saw the storm among us. However, we couldn't see all those changes until we looked back. Although we believed in the change as we drove forward. And fortunately for Tanya, she made it into *some* of my wildest dreams!

Shawn Foster

Cancer

> He is no fool who gives up what he cannot keep
> to gain what he cannot lose.
>
> ~Jim Eliot

*C*ancer? *I have cancer? I'm forty years old; how do I have cancer? How do I tell my wife? How do I tell my kids that Daddy might not be here next Christmas? How do I tell my mom? What about the school district? Cancer. God, what will I tell Tanya? There's no handbook for telling someone I might die.*

Driving from the ENT, I knew I must talk to Tanya, but I didn't know *how*. Who would? I'm never at a loss for words, but silence spoke loudly on that car ride. Before I turned on Route 1, my phone buzzed.

"Hey, sweetie."

"How did your appointment go?"

"It went well."

"What did he say?"

Beyond her voice, I heard tires rolling, and I quickly decided to postpone the inevitable. Since we were both driving, I figured an emotional crash could trigger a physical one.

"He said he'd let me know in a few days."

"So that's good?"

"It's indefinite. Nothing we can't handle. Probably sleep apnea—you know how these things go as we get older. Let's talk about it at home. I've got a busy day—lots of summer moves to make."

"Me too. I'm glad you went. I hope you didn't miss your lunch."

I'd forgotten lunch.

~

When Tanya and I settled the kids for the evening, I pulled her aside.

"I want to talk to you about something." My tone unsettled her, but I maintained composure and said matter-of-factly, "The doctor thinks I have cancer."

Her blank stare paused the clocks. I held my breath.

"Quit playing!" She gently slapped my thigh.

"I'm not playing. He's not sure, but he suspects it. He gave me his cell phone number and said we could call with questions."

The reality sucked the room breathless. We called the doctor, and the eventualities rushed upon us. *What if I? What if we? What do we tell?*

"Shawn, what do we tell the kids?"

"For now, nothing. We don't know anything. All we know are possibilities. Once we meet with the doctor, then we'll determine what to tell the kids."

Buying time feels harrowing when you don't know how much time you have left to spend. We felt like someone held down life's accelerator, and all we could do was brace our feet and cling to the seats. As parents, we paused externally but found difficulty when braking internally.

After we received the biopsy and CT scan results and the doctor confirmed our fears, we planned our next steps. Our upcoming family vacation to Disney World kicked off in one week, and the doctor granted us a reprieve until the Monday after the trip. When we returned, I'd have the chemo port and feeding tube inserted, so there was no turning back. Until then, the less the kids knew, the better.

"Tanya, I'll tell the kids after Disney World. I don't want them carrying all that baggage during our vacation. This could be our last one. God only knows, but I know I want us to enjoy this one."

"So, what are you going to tell them?"

"Nothing."

"No, what will you say if they ask if it's terminal?"

"I'm going to be Dad. I won't be a liar. I'll tell them I might not make it, that I might not be here."

That weight felt heavier when it left my mouth than it did in my head.

Shawn Foster

Time Out

Before a challenge, we have a plan. During a challenge, we find a purpose.

Time In

I'd heard people say, "When man makes plans, God laughs," but I'd never bought into it. I'd always felt like God gave me a mind so I could plan. I planned on telling my kids I may die. What I hadn't read at that time was, "Many are the plans in the mind of a man, but it is the purpose of the LORD that will stand."[11] I hadn't planned for that—I'd learn soon enough.

Despite our weighty baggage, we had a fantastic time at Disney World. Tanya and I occasionally stumbled—especially watching our kids' smiling faces—knowing what awaited us at home. In a day or so, we settled into the vacation and nearly forgot the impending storm. Those were wise choices. We could have spent those days drinking in sorrow; we chose to drink in laughter instead.

When we got home the rush returned, the pressure mounted, and the room shrank around us. One can only stave off a battle for so long, but the day comes when we must lean into it. We gathered in the living room, and I eased into the conversation.

"Well, tell me about Disney World. What was your favorite part?"

"My favorite part was all the characters. I never thought they'd seem so real!"

"My favorite part was that we got to skip the line!"

"Yeah, that may have been my favorite part, too."

"All right, what was your favorite food?"

I think I heard pizza or cotton candy, but the conversation playing in my mind blocked out the one in the living room.

"Hey, I've got something I need to tell you all."

Alyx's eyebrows darkened; Aden's rose. I hadn't allowed much transition time, and their antennas twitched.

"Your dad has cancer."

Call My Bluff

You know what that is, right? Cancer?"

Alyx nodded. I launched into a short explanation, speaking calmly and slowly, defusing the emotional tension. When I thought the worst had passed, Aden reeled me in.

"So, Daddy, you gonna die?"

I looked at Tanya, and she looked at me. The static room fell silent around us. We were caught between a truth and a lie. Tell the truth, and all hell will break loose. Tell a lie, and I become one if I die.

"So, Daddy, does that mean you're going to die?"

I took the plunge.

"Son, Daddy's going to be okay."

REMEMBER WHAT I WROTE ABOUT PLANS?

When Tanya and I convened in the bedroom, she questioned me with her eyes.

"I thought we had a plan. I thought you said you wouldn't be a liar."

"Sweetie, I'm asking God to save me so I'm not a liar to our children."

Faith

I had stepped into faith. That first step meant nothing and everything simultaneously. I'd stepped into faith, but I hadn't practiced it. Making the statement to trust God meant nothing; making the decision to practice it changed my world. **Step one: Trust God to heal me.** I had no contingency plans for when he didn't.

Shawn Foster

Substance

Someone once wrote, "Now faith is the substance of things hoped for . . ."[12] But when I looked around, I didn't see any substance. I saw Tanya, the kids, my job, and all the responsibility on my shoulders, and then I saw my diagnosis. Stage IV cancer. Survival rate: Abysmal. I'd taken a step of faith and sunk to the bottom. When I didn't know what to do, I turned to an age-old practice and called someone wiser than me: Pop.

Pop always seemed to have the answers. Often, in my darkest moments, I'd sneak off and call him. Many people can't wait to give you advice; Pop waited patiently for when I needed it most. When he gave it, he gave just enough, but never more than I could handle. He answered on the first ring.

"How are you feeling, son?"

"Pop, I'm down. Cancer. I don't know what to do."

"Shawn, everything you need, you already have."

Everything you need, you already have. Everything you need, you already have. Everything you need, you already have. **Step two: I took inventory.** What did I have?

- o I had youth.
- o I had good doctors.
- o I had a loving wife.
- o I had two great kids.
- o I had Mom in my corner.
- o I had Grandma and Pop.
- o I had good friends.
- o I had good mentors.
- o I had good colleagues.
- o I had Cyrus's voice in my ear.
- o I had experience winning.
- o I had overcome adversity.
- o I had persevered through tragedy.
- o I had much to live for.
- o I had faith.

And when I looked up, my faith had substance.

Evidence

That same author finished defining faith as "the evidence of things not seen." My faith needed evidence. I couldn't just "have faith" and sit around having it. What good is money that sits in the drawer until we die? I must practice it. I had to expend, which I did by following my doctor's advice. **Step three: I did something.** "You've got to show up."
 I told God, "I will show up. I will show up every day."
 Then I said to the cancer, "I will show up every day and show you that you can't beat me. I'm going to compete."
 My faith had evidence. One could see my footsteps to and from the cancer center. One could watch me vomit in trash cans and get right back up. One could hear me on my knees at night. I left DNA everywhere I went, but it had a new definition in this phase of my life. DNA: Do Not Accept.

Plans v. Purpose

I had plans; God had a purpose. I promised my children that I wouldn't die and asked God to help me keep it. I vowed to him, not knowing what I'd gotten myself into. I practiced my faith: I had substances and evidence and everything I needed all around me.
 But . . . what if God called my bluff?

Shawn Foster

Beside Myself

Chemotherapy is not for the faint of heart. Rather, it makes you faint of heart. It breaks your heart. It shoves you in the corner, exposing your weaknesses. It's war.

When I hobbled into the war room, patients huddled over trash cans, wiped away sweaty tears, and labored between chairs like prodded cattle. The clinical walls echoed muffled cries, and the acrid air smelled of disinfectant and vomit.

People were dying. But she was living. I never got her name, never thought to ask. During chemotherapy, I felt sicker than a dog. Again, I puked my guts out, tears stained my cheeks, and I could hardly walk. All of that weakness, and I was still young. She wasn't. An elderly White lady with no name but with a fresh spirit took chemotherapy weekly, and nobody could tell. Her wispy, white hair bounced when she talked, and her stained, crooked teeth brightened when she smiled. I know because she rarely stopped smiling. She'd take her treatment and say, "Well, I guess I'll do a little shopping now."

Shopping? I can't even walk to the bathroom.

I overheard her say she'd taken chemotherapy for eleven years. Eleven years! This lady hopped around like someone half her age *while* she took chemotherapy. I never saw her have one side effect. None. She came, took her poison, and left. I looked for a lasso of truth, but I never saw one, just a smile and a wave, a hop, a skip, and a jump into the sunshine. Meanwhile, I was dying.

I'd mentally reviewed my prognosis until I'd reached utter exhaustion. I had next to no chance of making it. My spirits hit a new low, but desperation can weave into others' hearts and cry for help. Or

Knee Deep

faith spots desperation far off and rushes in to save. Either way, the next time I saw her, she had a word for me.

"I've been thinking about you."

Wiping my mouth with my sleeve, I said, "Oh yeah?"

"A thought and a spirit came to me and said, 'He's going to be okay.'"

I looked at her through mirrored eyes, and she continued, "So, I got you something that reminds me of you. I think of you often."

I didn't know this lady's name, and she had something for me? She thought of me often? I wanted to retreat into a turtle shell, and at that moment, I'm sure I looked like it. With the bit of strength I had, I held out a brittle hand, and she handed me her gift. I unfolded the gray t-shirt, and in black ink was written WARRIOR.

Time Out

Warrior? Have you ever seen an emaciated man whose sunken eyes may roll out of his head, hunched over a trash can, heaving snot and tears and sweat? It's not pretty. Warrior? The grim reaper overshadowed my body like a dark vulture awaiting my last heartbeat. Warrior? I didn't look like a warrior. I looked like a prisoner of war.

Time In

Before I could thank her, she said, "This is who you are. So make sure you *be* who you *are*."

I held my head high. "I'll remember. I'll remember who I am."

Warriors and Prisoners of War

That sprightly lady gave me insight into myself: She became my two-way mirror. I couldn't see out, but she could see in. If I could have sat beside myself and taken a look, I would have realized that I'd become a prisoner of war. Now, a prisoner can be a warrior, but a warrior can't be a prisoner. A true warrior may be imprisoned, but in his heart, his warrior fire still burns. I'd become a prisoner of war. I'd nearly given up, but a guardian angel draped me in new armor that read WARRIOR across the chest. Because of that transaction, I remembered who I was, and I became an imprisoned warrior—not a prisoner of war. I may have been imprisoned in my body, but my spirit roamed freely. Although I surrendered to my treatment, I hadn't been defeated.

Surrender and Defeat

I must caution that *there's a marked difference between surrendering and defeat.* Warriors surrender when it's wise to do so. But that doesn't mean they're defeated. Far from it. Some warriors wait weeks, months, and even years, seeking the precise moment to strike. Escape lingers in their hearts. Though their ragged bodies hover near death, their spirits live. They see beyond the bars.

Begrudge or Behold

As a forty-year-old male who had been a collegiate athlete, I could have begrudged that lady's vibrancy or envied her buoyant spirit. While she bounced like a spry chicken—no, I don't mean spring chicken—I could have grown annoyed and pushed her away. I had the choice to sneer and begrudge her joy or marvel at her spirit and enjoy. Understanding the difference was paramount.

Good leaders experience vicariously. The term *vicarious* gets a bad rap. We often imagine a beer-bellied dad screaming while his son pitches sorely from the mound. We judge the father for intertwining his personal value with his son's independent performance. The dad seems childish. Although the dad is living vicariously, he's doing it with a bullish view.

Yet, in another part of town, a maestro conducts a symphony, and the pitches and falls elevate near a crescendo, and we catch our fingers moving rhythmically like we're playing upright bass. We don't judge that action harshly, but in that moment, *we* live vicariously. We are not only enjoying the show; we are actively participating in it, imagining ourselves as a key member. That's not bad; that's good. I doubt anyone ever judges an air guitar-playing child for mimicking his favorite band. And if a heartless, joy-killing soul does judge a child for that, then we should assume that judge must begrudge.

Now, why would I bring this up? Because the difference between a leader who begrudges and a leader who beholds is the difference between a bully and a believer. Bullies mandate a performance for *their* enjoyment. Bullies don't care about you. If you fail to please a bully, he gets angry; if you continue to fail, he gets even. Your failure hurts his self-confidence, and he's so insecure he must hurt you to make himself feel even. Now, imagine the dad screaming at his son.

> Ball one: "Throw it over the plate, Billy."
> Ball two: "What are you doing?!"
> Ball three: "You throw like a *girl!*"
> Ball four: "I don't know whose son you are because I didn't teach you to throw like that!"

Bullies attack a victim's self-identity when their self-identity feels shattered. They're living vicariously in its worst form.

On the other hand, a believer beholds your life testimony and *chooses* when to join in. Sometimes, believers watch and applaud; other times, they strum along. During my cancer treatments, I couldn't sing, dance, or throw baseballs with my son. In my weakened state, I could only imagine. When my T-shirt-giving muse smiled and laughed, I joined in her joy because it helped me and her. It helped *us*. It gave us hope. It allowed us to express ourselves. Please understand that I didn't do the work; I just followed along. Had I begrudged her, I would have denied myself vicarious joy, and I would have denied her blessing. And I wouldn't have this cool T-shirt. Remember, "Envy rots the bones."[13]

As leaders, we allow people their personal spice, join their experiences when it serves them, allow them to be great, and never use their greatness against them. If we spend it on ourselves, we've stolen it. I'll land the plane with this: If we begrudge a person's joy, what does that say about us?

Shawn Foster

Defeat and Surrender

We've all heard the adage, "There's a difference between giving up and giving in." There probably is, but at some point, we enter a semantics battle that results in very little real-life change. However, I must draw a dividing line between the ideas of defeat and surrender. I touched on this earlier, but it needs a second, third, and fourth treatment until all the evidence of cancerous thinking is gone.

To surrender is to give up control—which we never had in the first place. If we surrender, we yield to an emotion, influence, or situation. As my cancer progressed, I yielded much. I comprehended that without chemotherapy, I would die. I also surrendered control of outcomes. Chemo may save me, wreck me, or both. And, it did. I surrendered in hopes of recovery. I did not accept defeat.

Defeat indicates losing, failure, and termination. Like surrender, defeat is an event. Unlike surrender, defeat intimates permanence. Once we lose a battle, that battle is permanently over—we're defeated. If we fight again, we fight a *new* battle. Defeat is a one-time loss.

Here's the difference. When we say, "Cancer defeated him," we're saying he died. However, if we say, "He surrendered to cancer," we're saying he relinquished control—we don't know the final outcome yet.

Let's try both in a hypothetical situation. Cancer defeated Shawn, but Shawn still won the battle. That's a contradiction. How could Shawn lose and win? Now, let's try the other. Shawn surrendered to cancer, but Shawn still won the battle. That's not a contradiction. We understand something happened between the surrender and the victory. Surrender leaves room for escape, and surrender leaves room for mercy. When we suffer defeat, the victor has shown no mercy.

Surrender

I surrendered. I fought cancer tooth and nail until the dog didn't have any fight left. What could he do, gum it to death? I recognized the disconnect between my broken body and warrior spirit: my body failing, my spirit strong. I was okay with that. I could lose my body without losing my self-respect. I could lose my body without losing myself. I could lose my body and win my spirit: by faith, I could become the man I always wanted to be. I offered my body to the mercy of another.

Shawn Foster

Death

On September 10, I gathered my family and told them the news. They had watched my skin grow looser and my veins thinner. A stumble or fall no longer registered as an incident but a daily occurrence, like closing the cabinet door or opening a window. My palpable weakness sent a message nobody wanted to believe, one that we all saw with our eyes but denied with our hearts.

As a husband and a father, I couldn't allow us to continue that way. We must step from the denial and face the reality before us, so I gathered everyone together and said, "I don't think your dad's going to beat this cancer thing."

We dropped tears of plenty and still clung to what we wanted to be true, but I knew false expectations bore resentment's scars. "And I'm okay with that." I reassured them that I wasn't "okay" leaving them, but if my number were called, I was convinced God would care for them and me, too. We ached and cried and mourned, and I surrendered. I accepted my death as inevitable, and I gave my future over to God. I put it in his hands.

If he chose to save me, I'd accept it, and if he chose to let me die, I'd accept that, too. Even if he let me die, wouldn't he do something with my spirit? Couldn't I face death fearlessly because he had prepared for it? I got knee-deep and prayed, "I'm okay—I'm not going to do anything to fix it. I'm going to follow your lead."

That crucial moment changed me. I died to my fears. I no longer feared losing my job, inadequacy, or others' opinions. I realized that betraying my conscience to gain others' favor gained me nothing. It only cost me. If I died, their favor wouldn't come with me, but my conscience would. And my conscience would meet my Maker.

Around the corner lurked death's door, and I must keep walking. I trusted God to handle what was on the other side. I opened the door and stepped through.

I died. I died to myself, and then I fell asleep.

Starting Over; Starting New

"Get up, son, it's time to get up. You've got to walk through the house and go to work. Shawn, you hear me? It's time to get up."

Mom? Is it New Year's? No, that's not Mom. Go to work? I must be dreaming. How am I going to do this? I haven't been to work in two months. I've lost sixty-five pounds. My clothes don't fit. I've got this feeding tube, and my esophagus is on fire. How will I get up?

I swung both feet over the side of the bed and dropped them to the floor like I had a thousand times before. I stood up and moved one step at a time, telling Tanya, "I'm going to work today," though she looked at me with disbelieving eyes. I tapped my feeding tube, Old Faithful, and remembered that feelings of inadequacy most deeply test our valiance, so I walked to the restroom with my head held high. I could not allow insecurity to override my duty. I dressed in old clothes, kept from a skinnier time, and though I looked like death, I felt a new life.

How will I get up? "The same way you have thousands of times before, Shawn."

How will I get up? "A new way you have never tried before, Shawn."

I started over, but this time without fear. What's left to fear when you don't fear death? I went to work and had the best day I could. No magic beans sprouted; no rainbows greeted me when Tanya dropped me off near the door. But as the day wore on, I felt my strength increase. Even as my body weakened, my *resolve* grew. My heart grew stronger.

That night, as Tanya and I shared an evening conversation, I used my classic line. "*I want to tell you something.* As I walked into work today, a thought came to me: 'Time doesn't belong to you. You may want to put a period on your life, but really what you experienced was a comma. It was just a pause.'

"Now I understand why people say, 'You must practice faith.' I thought it was over, but I got one more day. I could have stayed in bed believing God might have healed me since I didn't die, but going to work was my practice. That was the only way my faith would improve."

Death and Rebirth

I cannot overemphasize this enough: The great freedom I enjoyed after dying to myself didn't come from dying. It came while living. Death served as the cause, the event that opened a new life's door, but living made the difference. I *felt* free when I went to bed unafraid to die on September 10, but I *experienced* freedom when I faced the next day.

We often overserve death and underserve resurrection. We glamorize sacrifice but disdain mercy. I'd given everything I had, sacrificed my life, and it wasn't enough! Only God's mercy allowed me to live. It wasn't just accepting death that changed my life; it was falling on God's mercy. Two parts: truth and grace.

We can hear, "You must die to yourself," without much effect because dying is only half the experience. When I stopped fearing death, when I died to myself, it changed my perspective. And when my perspective changed, my thinking changed, and I was reborn. My natural thesis changed from fear-based to faith-based. The second half of the experience came when I practiced my faith daily.

Birth brings new life into the world, but a new baby doesn't learn to walk solely because she has been born. She must learn to take steps. The same proved true for me. I'd died to myself, but when I got my new lease on life, I had to learn to walk. I didn't learn to walk again; I learned to walk a new way.

And I learned something about faith. It's not a one-and-done, shot-in-the-arm type of substance. Faith requires time, thought, and experience. Just like I'd learned to fear others' opinions, barking dogs, or drowning, I learned to trust God—to do as he saw fit. I couldn't gain it all in one day: One day served as a turning point, and every day served as a learning point.

I still had fear. I still had to relinquish control and lean into faith. I still had to practice. With fear, we often don't realize *when* we're practicing because it's our natural thesis. Once we've changed our natural thesis, we must learn to scoot, crawl, and walk in it, and we must realize that we can fall. But understanding we can fall doesn't mean we fear falling: It means we accept that falling is possible; we comprehend relapse is probable; we no longer live in denial; instead, we face our fears. A bird trained to fly down can still fly up. A man trained to walk by faith can still fall into fear, especially when he quits training. It's how the world works.

I can't run one mile and be fit forever. I can't eat one salad and be nourished forever. I can't trust one time and remain faithful forever. I practice daily because gravity, self-consumption, and fear do not terminate. So, neither can I.

A Wish and a Prayer

I can honestly say, "I wish I had cancer earlier." The experience taught me perseverance, surrender, and faith. I persevered through the dark days and the hopeful ones. I surrendered to God, and he gave me mercy: He let me die to myself, my control, and my fear. He gave me a new life by challenging me to walk in faith. On September 11, 2018, I returned to work. Every day after that, I improved, and at my next physical exam, they deemed me cancer-free. I've been cancer-free ever since. I even got to ring the bell. But only after I'd rung the death knell over my old life.

Shawn Foster

Ring the Bell

I got to ring the bell when the oncologists declared me cancer-free. I shook the hell out of that bell. I'm a laid-back guy, maybe even stoic at times, but I nearly broke my face smiling while I rang the cancer-free bell.

> **Progress Update**
>
> We must ring the bell. We'll learn to celebrate, and then we'll turn our attention to facing new challenges. After a victory, another battle awaits, but for a brief moment, we all must celebrate.

Whoever inaugurated the cancer-free bell-ringing ceremony must have understood our deeply human need to reinforce belief with reward. People need something to believe in and something to be rewarded for. That cancer-free bell symbolizes an accomplishment; its toll echoes a story of freedom—another person conquered cancer—that's a reward! In their hearts, they believed that deliverance lay somewhere in the distant future, maybe somewhere they couldn't see, but somewhere they could hear when another survivor rang the bell. That's something to believe in. That ringing sound is beautiful, for it's the sound of belief realized—the evidence of things not yet seen.

- Belief = Other people have rung the bell, so can I.
- Reward = I will ring the bell if I continue to fight.

See, belief heals like medicine. That's why placebos work. And when we couple our belief that something works with our hope for a tangible outcome, our chances of success skyrocket. I'm not saying only believe and don't take your medicine; I am saying your medicine works better if you believe it works. We don't have a guarantee, but believe me, we do have a reward to seek.

When we complete an important task, it's important to celebrate. The celebration reinforces a job well done and inspires us to face our next adversity. Since we are all individuals, the level to which we celebrate must be highly individualized. The frequency and fervor with which we celebrate is up to us. Some dance after every first down; others smile when they cash their check.

As leaders, we must allow others to celebrate their wins with and without us. We can do the work, lead the way, get them there, and then politely step aside while they ring the bell. We don't need to participate in every parade we create, but we do need to create parades.

Contrary to my previous point, celebrating every step can be overkill. Every email, every conversation, every first down doesn't require a celebration dance. Actually, that devalues the true celebration. But again, as leaders, we must allow for individuality. Again, our job is to know *when*.

After every chemo treatment, I celebrated that I made it, but I didn't ring the bell. I celebrated my arrival by plopping my butt in the chair and taking the treatment that killed and saved me simultaneously. I wanted to ring the bell, thought about ringing the bell, imagined ringing the bell, but I withheld the bell ringing. I reserved the bell ringing for the end.

Time Out

Some cancer survivors fight *just* to ring the bell. Just like salespeople work around the clock to win a $20 medal at an award ceremony, cancer survivors scratch and claw for the bell. Personal survival rings hollow for them, but ringing the bell becomes their reason for living. The same may be true for us and those we lead. Sometimes, we'll fight harder for the celebratory award than we will for the work. And discerning leaders recognize motivations. If we listen, people will tell us. So let the reward

Shawn Foster

seekers know they'll get to ring the bell when they win. And be sure to ring the bell when you win, too.

Time In

When you win, ring the bell. When others win, have them ring the bell. When you're seeking a win, tell everyone about the bell. Let the bell ringers come to you. Practice ringing the bell, for you never know when your name will be called.

I rang the bell on the bus as a child. That experience inflated my desire to ring the bell. I felt responsible. In the same way, I wanted to ring the cancer-free bell. I'd tasted the responsibility as a child, and as an adult, it all came clanging back. We never know how one celebration as a child will prepare us for a trial as an adult.

Be vigilant. Your next bell-ringer is waiting around the corner, ready to wallop you upside the head. To avoid getting your bell rung, you better duck.

Bridging the Gap

Before cancer invaded my life, I pushed through an adversarial experience that nearly destroyed my belief in mankind's goodness. I'd been uniquely convinced that humans, at our core, were innately good; however, this ongoing dogfight almost convinced me otherwise. Almost.

Dr. Sean Alford and I were hired as the superintendent and deputy superintendent of schools in Aiken, South Carolina, and we immediately initiated changes. From the first moment, we spearheaded initiatives that forever changed the lives of students. We raised the graduation rate from 82.7 percent to 91 percent. Not only did we improve the graduation rate, but we also gave the community safe, effective, and inviting learning environments of which it could be proud. It turned out some community members didn't want that. They wanted things to go back to the way they were.

Consequently, making changes stretched our tenacity like thin-skinned rubber bands, begging us to cry, "Uncle!" Ironically, we initiated the changes, but the initiated changes nearly broke us. But as life goes, it wasn't so ironic after all, since we birth change in our mind's ecstasy but bear it out through our body's industry. Maybe we just didn't know what we had gotten ourselves into. Bringing change to life in Aiken mirrored the birthing process: It started in pain!

Humans often operate in denial. I suppose that's how a mother convinces herself that another childbirth won't be so bad. Denial is powerful. However, if we want change, we must face our denial.

Facing denial requires grit and is a two-step process. First, we must comprehend that what's before us, in us, and around us is not as we want it. That's problem identification. However, any cynic can identify a problem, and it takes action to solve one. That's step two: Take action. To face denial, we must step into it, not just notice it and throw our hands up.

As part of the labor process and the change process, contractions come. It's insufficient to say, "I'm having contractions," and do nothing. Change comes quickly, so we must do something. The pain warns us.

In Aiken, we had overcrowded schools in one area and underutilized buildings in another. The demographics and the population concentration had changed, but the district hadn't. You've got to understand that when change doesn't look like what we expect, we tend to deny it. Since the population concentration shifted, but the population didn't increase, many disregarded the change. This sounds ridiculous, but that's akin to saying a mom holding a newborn and a pregnant lady fill equal amounts of space, so no changes are needed around the house.

To be fair, many community members saw the need and wanted change. That's why Sean and I got hired. Also, many still support those changes and are my great friends, so don't let my story of some make you judge all. I don't name names, and I don't disparage people, but I do call a ball foul when it scatters outside the lines.

Back to the baby analogy. Biology announces a baby is coming, yet many young expecting couples still function in denial. They fail to prepare. Biology kicks the door in. They fail to "nest." Contractions begin. Some still procrastinate. *Gas, maybe? Who knows?* Maybe the soon-to-be mother's biology malfunctioned, or the father's hyperactive denial took over. It doesn't matter; the baby is on its way, and early labor has begun.

We made cuts and consolidated schools; we had to. To say a few schools underperformed would be a euphemism. Fourteen of our forty-two schools received a below-average or unsatisfactory grade via the state's rating scale. That's 33 percent! If you had three children, which one would you choose to receive a subpar education? Imagine selling our quality education to a new community member: "Not only does your child have a one-in-three shot at a below-average education, but at least the facilities are dilapidated, too."

What would you expect a new leadership team to do? We bulldozed the roadblocks. In our community, many didn't connect underperforming schools to raggedy-ass facilities (pardon my language). Some thought "below average" meant not too bad. "Cs get degrees," they said from outside the school walls. Honestly, most didn't look at the grades anyway; they said, "Things have always been this way. If it ain't broke, then don't fix it." Even though some schools received the "unsatisfactory" label, Sean and I had to make compelling arguments that *environments influence learning.* We pushed for new facilities. I suppose they wanted the water to break first.

Each woman experiences labor uniquely: That's why mothers can share birth stories, and no two will sound the same. One mother may rush to the hospital, push three times, and hold her new baby within two hours, while another labors for two days, never pushes, and passes out after the cesarean section. Despite individual experiences, birth follows a process: early labor, active labor, birth/delivery, placenta delivery, and recovery. Yet, trivializing birth into a cookie-cutter process is foolish; however—and this is a very important *however*—planning for the birth process is wise! Individuality does not license ignorance; it liberates exploration. In simple English, just because you don't know how something will happen doesn't make it okay to ignore it.

Sean and I planned. We explored our options. Change was imminent. We conducted population and demographic studies, hired consultants to do the same, initiated multiple town hall meetings with individual communities, and met with the board and advisory councils. We'd have purchased the car seat before the second trimester!

Time Out

In Aiken, we have school boards and advisory councils written into our laws. So, to effect change in a school district, a superintendent must secure a school board's majority vote and *should* receive the advisory council's confidence. Advisory councils do not make policy, but analogous to a two-parent home where one parent exercises authority and the other exercises influence, it's always better to secure the blessing of both. This meant our leadership team had more than our fair share of people to please.

Shawn Foster

Time In

We initiated Aiken's first bond referendum in forty-two years. Our research concluded that we must build and consolidate (through rezoning) to best serve our students. Tempers flared, and we moved from early labor to active labor. We heard some grumbling in the hills.

"We don't need new schools. Our population's not increasing."

"We don't want to rezone our kids from one school to another. It'll disrupt their families."

"We don't need more money. Just spend our money more wisely."

Those weren't inaccurate grumblings. In fact, we agreed. The population hadn't increased; it shifted.

Rezoning students disrupts families and so does receiving an unsatisfactory education. Rezoning, if done correctly, improves the lives of students and families more than it disrupts them. If you had a gang-infested emergency room next door or a state-of-the-art one a mile away, which would you choose?

Finally, we wholeheartedly agreed with the financial complaints. Good stewardship required that we spend our money wisely: If we discontinued dumping money into money-pit facilities and built new ones while consolidating others to maximize efficacy, we could move to a 24-1 student-to-teacher ratio. Keeping the status quo, we had a 12-1 ratio in some schools and 36-1 in others. In our plans, the student population remained the same, but the facility population decreased—lowering overall costs. And, concerning classroom sizes, when we subtracted the twelve students from the classes of thirty-six students, we found our 33 percent!

But as we met, and reasoned, and pushed, the contractions heightened. We heard all types of deliberations, but a few true contentions went unsaid: "Johnny went to Chukker Creek Elementary School, so we want Timmy to go to Chukker Creek Elementary School, too. Even if it's falling apart and keeps our students at a statewide disadvantage, it's more important to us that Timmy and Johnny have the same mascot than for everyone to receive an improved education." Or, "If you build new schools, our small community will lose its community school, and we'd rather students suffer in *our* community than excel in *another*." Even if that community existed right around the corner.

> GOOD LEADERS DON'T GIVE UP 50 PERCENT
> OF $1 MILLION TO GET 100 PERCENT OF $10.

The labor pains increased. Our mild contractions that accompanied legitimate concerns transformed into harsh ones. Early on, the complaints helped us fine-tune our process. They didn't serve ill purposes; they served good purposes. They forced our leadership team to refine our plans and ensure superior service for all. But when the labor increased, our water broke and out flowed the torrent of accusations.

Let's recall the Narrative Intimidation Process:

1. *You* are not committed; *you* are not one of us.
2. *You* are not trustworthy; *you* are a cheater or liar.
3. *You* don't have the money, power, or pull to do what *you* say.
4. *You* are going to get fired!

We got pummeled all at once. Although Sean often played the bad cop, and I played the good one, we both weathered severe scrutiny—his worse than mine. Let's be clear about accusation number one: We were outsiders, and we were not one of them yet. We'd both been newly hired and, frankly, we were both African American. I'm not making this a race thing; I'm just pointing out a fact. The two highest-ranking educational officials in Aiken were African American, but only 32 percent of the population was African American. Had I been another race, no problem. If Sean had been another race, even better. But as it was, people followed the false narrative process.

At this point, I could repeat the mind-numbingly derogatory insults, violent threats, false accusations, or employment threats levied at us, but for what purpose? With a finger snap and a keyboard tap, we could move from informational to inflammatory. However, as leaders, we must understand that when pushed, people resort to guerilla warfare. We don't have to. *The acts of a few don't represent the majority view*—they just tip the scales.[14]

During the upheaval, many community, board, and advisory council members behaved above board. We had a helpful dialogue and stressed finding the best possible solution. Again, *the few* didn't. *The few* violated, threatened, bullied, excoriated, and accused. According to *the few*, Sean and I embezzled district money, spent it on our girlfriends, and planned to skip town once we secured the bond referendum—in our pockets. Can you imagine what Tanya would do to me if I even *thought* about having a girlfriend?

If we succumbed to the character assassination and quit, we'd confirm the baseless claims, but if we stood fast against them, we'd confirm them with our denial. *The few* expect you to deny defamation and use your denial to confirm your guilt. Think of the Salem witch trials. Wouldn't a witch claim not to be a witch? To secure her freedom, she must confess to being bewitched into witchery. We didn't have that option. So, what did we do? We pushed right—through . . . the . . . pain—can you see the baby's head yet?

At the contractions' height, we pushed. We rallied support for the referendum and met in schools, churches, and restaurants to advocate for kids. We cast our vision far and deep and inspired many community members, and then tragedy struck.

Crisis

On Friday, January 27, 2017, after a basketball game at Aiken High School, mayhem ensued. While dining near the school, I saw blue lights blaze by. Immediately, I received a call that someone had been shot outside the gym. I rushed to the scene and worked with our crisis response team. With the law enforcement officers, we blockaded the area to ensure safety, communicated with the families of the students on campus, and got the students home safely. A person had shot three individuals outside the gym. Two were students. None were fatally wounded. For privacy's sake, I will not use names. It was awful.

Sean had visited a conference in Philadelphia that weekend, so I manned the helm. We enacted our crisis response plan, but the plan failed to fully address an after-school hours shooting involving adults, students, community members, etc. No matter how I sliced it, it haunted me. We weren't responsible, but we also weren't prepared. I promise that *we learned the lesson.*

A few months later, amid the accusations and name-calling, I'd had enough. My beliefs hung like torn sheets over a clothesline, clothespins falling to the ground. I thought about giving up. That day, I sat at the kitchen table holding my face in my hands when Tanya walked in. I heard her footsteps and said, "I don't think I want to do this anymore. I don't have a problem with education—I don't know if I want to be in leadership anymore." I lifted my eyes. "I knew people would say and do unkind things, but I always believed people were good at their core. Now, I'm not so sure. I hung my hat on the belief that when people did terrible things, something terrible must have happened to them. But for this past week, I've wondered if people do evil things because we are evil. Are we more bad than good?"

My question hung like a forgotten ghost searching for validation. Just before the wisps blew away, Tanya responded. "You have an opportunity. When you encounter someone who seems bad to their core, show them what good *is*. If you respond appropriately rather than to the way they're behaving, maybe you'll teach them what good is."

I took Tanya's advice, and circumstances improved. When individuals approached me vindictively, I extended the olive branch. This often unsettled them and momentarily beset the vitriol. As I behaved kindly, it slowly changed their behavior. Some continued to assault, some stopped, and some even mirrored my behavior.

In November 2017, we passed the initial bond referendum, and in May 2018, we passed our second bond referendum. The baby had been born! We had the means to welcome it appropriately. Then, the real work began. We had to *raise the child.* We constructed, consolidated, improved, and reduced, and, to top it all off, the placenta came rushing out. I got diagnosed with cancer.

Shawn Foster

Bridging the Gap 2.0

Describing my battle with cancer has proven difficult. At times, I liken it to a swimmer undulating just above the waves, barely keeping his nose above water. Other times, I compare it to riding a bronco; when the wild ride ended, I looked beaten half-to-death. I believe my best metaphor is breaking in a baseball glove: Although it broke me down, I learned when to be pliable and where to never break. Nearly dying delineated my nonnegotiables and my reasonable doubts.

On this side of chemotherapy, the intensity increased when community members launched a full-scale attack on Sean. This pigeonholed me into a precarious situation for three reasons: One, I discovered my true allies during my cancer treatment—and some of them stood against Sean. Two, I stood by Sean's decisions. Three, I was also named Shawn.

When I lay face-down in the dirt, beaten by cancer, many neighbors, friends, and family members pitched in. We had gift baskets and gift cards and gift meals for weeks—so many reasons to be grateful. Unexpectedly, we received mounds of gifts from people we hardly knew, friends of friends, people we'd call acquaintances.

People I'd met once or twice offered transportation to and from chemotherapy. Tanya received gifts from church members she'd never met. My kids got cards and money from people whose last names didn't register on our cell phones. Kindness poured in, and it took an army to keep up with the "get well soon" cards. My mind reembraced humanity's inherent goodness.

And then *the few* dumped on that. Residents fired false accusations at Sean. They accused him of swindling funds from educational accounts to cover personal costs; they accused him of playing favorites.

Knee Deep

They accused him of threatening an employee. What was I to do? I'd worked beside him for four years, seen no flaky skin, and we had made massive improvements together. They had the wrong guy, and I felt contempt toward *the few*. Was levying false accusations enough to destroy my faith in humanity's goodness? Maybe I took their attacks on him too personally. However, character assassination usually assassinates more than a person's character. It assassinates lives. False accusations lead to uprisings that destroy entire communities. Ask Emperor Nero. They planted doubting seeds, and doubting seeds create conspiracies. But *what if what they said was true?*

I addressed their statements. "I'm sure your concerns are valid, but is your evidence? Everyone may rightfully concern themselves with educational matters, but nobody rightfully states suspicions as evidence. I give you respect, and I expect you to respect Sean until proven otherwise."

I answered angry citizens the way I wanted to be answered: respectfully, with facts, and with a charge to do the same. Like Tanya said, "When you think someone is bad at their core, maybe you need to show them *good*." I modeled the behavior I expected, and in some cases, it worked. That was a light in the darkness. However, I still had a conundrum. Many of Sean's objectors had proven invested acquaintances during my cancer. How do you tell someone who's proven their love to you to "piss off" in favor of another who's proven their love to you?

I didn't mix apples and oranges. How people treated me created zero gravitas when it came to Sean. We can be sinister in the streets and kind behind closed doors and vice versa. Decisions are made by individuals, and considering an individual's behavior in one arena doesn't play well with considering their decisions in another. Again, I'd worked alongside Sean for four years. I didn't see any evidence of evil, but I sure saw plenty of good.

We'd made great strides, but if we didn't continue delivering after the bond election, then we truly would be fraudulent. Securing a passing vote required painful labor, but raising the baby would be much more difficult. I survived the placenta delivery; we stopped talking and started doing.

Shawn Foster

We had already reengineered our protocols and procedures to increase learning, and we had substantially cut our operational costs, which elevated our credit rating. After deploying technological upgrades to the facilities we retained, we also built new ones, razed old ones, and shifted the zoned population so that we level-loaded classrooms. Throughout this period, we completed fifteen building projects and negotiated land acquisitions, contract services, and government and business partnerships. None of that made a difference without results.

Remember, 33 percent of our schools had a below-average or unsatisfactory rating. After our changes, that number decreased to 2.4 percent, with zero unsatisfactory schools. Zero. After all was said and done, one school remained below average. Given more time, we would have fixed that one, too.

So, when agitators railed on and on about Sean, what could I do? I could protect mine and throw him under the school bus, or I could stand tall beside him. I chose to stand tall.

Quick Tips

> ➤ Suspicions are not evidence.
> ➤ Good people behaving badly is still bad.
> ➤ Character decisions are easy when we're unbeholden to others.

Understand that when I fought cancer, I fought with my back pinned against the wall. I had no way out but to go through, and by giving the results over to God, I learned that my character mattered more than my reputation, which was just other people's opinions of me anyway. I'd become like that broken-in baseball glove, deeper in the pocket.

I stood beside Sean. He took so much heat. We made it to step four in the narrative process, and *the few* threatened his job. Remember, *like a rudder turns a ship, the few navigate the many.* I saw the writing on the wall. No matter what improvements we made, when residents decided to hold their $10—their broken-down community schools and operations—rather than share $1 million with others, what could we do? They had become *fixed*. Someone needed to loosen them up.

My childhood friends had bought a peculiar-smelling substance. They lathered their baseball gloves with neatsfoot oil to soften the leather. Then, they stuffed two baseballs in the webbing, wrapped the glove in rubber bands, and let it take shape. When it finished, *presto*! They had a pliable glove with a deep pocket, one that could absorb a line drive without breaking their hand.

In our community, *the few* forgot to lube up before the game and grew so fixated on their desires that they dropped the ball, kicking away the change. C-rated schools suited them just fine, though the difference between a C- and a B+ may be the difference between a smelly bathroom and getting stabbed in the bathroom. I know that's inflammatory, but let's get real: We already had two students shot outside a high school basketball game! *Environment impacts education.* It's hard to learn when you're afraid to breathe. *Some* communities were unsafe, and we had the responsibility to impact the lives of *all* our students inside those communities. Our humanity requires we provide safe learning environments, and student safety is nonnegotiable.

Apparently, superintendent safety is not. They pushed Sean out—I heard it from my daughter's lips.

Often, people confused Sean and me, so we'd get credited and blamed for each other's actions. We even changed my title to reduce the confusion. I became the chief officer for operations and student services instead of the deputy superintendent. We made that decision early on, primarily so the only African Americans in advanced leadership weren't the only "supers" in the district. People get uptight about titles. It didn't matter. As I said, my daughter told me.

Alyx came home from school. "Daddy, a kid at school said, 'I heard your dad is getting fired.'"

"Kids say mean things, Alyx. Don't pay any attention to it. Sean Alford's job is up for review. They've got the wrong Shawn."

And those were the postpartum contractions. *The few* pushed Sean out. We should have celebrated our district's success and rang the "happy baby" bell, but instead, someone slapped the mother for getting pregnant. Sean was hired to make a change and then fired when they realized a new baby changed things.

Shawn Foster

This is where it all comes together. After birthing a baby and delivering a placenta, we must focus on restitution: restorative order. Change stretches us in ways we never intended, and sometimes, we need an episiotomy afterward. At a minimum, we all need recovery. Sean never got to do that. He brought change to life in our district, and at the appointed time, someone snatched away his chance to put neatsfoot oil on scuffed skin. They'd rather scab.

Choices

Dying taught me that he who sells what he can't keep to gain what he can't lose is wise. The time came for me to sell out. I got offered the superintendent's job, which came with a substantial raise. Substantial is an understatement. A salary increase creates an exponential long-term impact for educators in South Carolina. We base our retirement income on an educator's five highest consecutive years of earnings.

After working twenty-three years in education and as a forty-four-year-old man who had escaped the projects, pioneered my way through college athletics, earned three advanced degrees, provided for my family, and heard Cyrus bet me I could be a superintendent in such a large district, what do you think I did?

Bridging the Gap 3.0

I said no because I stood by Sean's decisions. I said no because I made the same decisions he did. I said no because we drastically improved the lives of children. I said no because the reward for a job well done is not to steal the job from the one who led you there. I said no because I realized that job performance does not provide protection, but God does. And for me to feel like I honored God's decision to spare my life, I couldn't say yes.

You've heard it said, "We need to keep the main thing the main thing," well, I say, "Doing the work is the main thing." Getting paid is not the main thing. Would you only change your child's diaper if you got paid? Becoming popular is not the main thing. Isn't Charles Ponzi's last name famous? Landing a promotion is not the main thing. Do we trust all our politicians who've been promoted to the highest levels? Regardless of how you answered those questions, for me, we did the work, so we did the main thing. How could I look myself in the eyes and capitalize on Sean's ousting when he did the main thing?

You've heard it said, "We have to take what we can get." Well, I say, "Everything that comes to you is not *for* you." You don't own it all, and you can't trust it all. Favorable conditions and fair-weather friends oscillate in the wind, but trustworthy companions stand by until the end.

Digression

Don't get lost in the weeds. We can see both Sean and some of *the few* supported me during my cancer treatments. They "stood by until the end." But one party's loyalty doesn't constitute overriding what's right. Cyrus could have offered me the job; Tanya could have begged me to take it, and I wouldn't have. Everything that comes to me is not for me—sometimes, it's a distraction.

How We Play the Game

You've heard it said, "Nobody remembers second place," but I say, "People remember notability, not first place." Do you remember who won the most recent fencing Olympic gold medal? I bet you remember who assassinated Abraham Lincoln. Do you remember who rode their way to gold in Dressage? I bet you don't even know what Dressage is. The Buffalo Bills lost four consecutive Super Bowls. Do you remember who won them?

What's my point? The reasoning behind "Nobody remembers second place" creates all sorts of maladapted practices. First, it's not true. Second place matters. Second is the second-best person in the competition, and that really matters when you discover the guy in first place took performance-enhancing drugs. Think Tour de France.

Second, we remember notability: famous and infamous. Again, Tour de France. We don't remember who won Olympic gold in the 100-meter dash four years before Jesse Owens at the 1936 Berlin Olympics. So, why do we remember his four gold medals? Because he won our hearts—he won notability. I bet we also remember who was hailed as Chancellor in Berlin, Germany, at those Olympics. He crushed our hearts—he earned his infamy.

Finally, when we focus on first place only, we lose sight. Competitors or friends fail to be people and become either impediments or proponents. Everything becomes about us. We become self-centered. We lose the *we*, and only *I* matter. And if I'm not first, I suppose I don't even matter. What should I do with some*thing* that no longer matters?

I didn't need to be first the way they wanted to give it to me. Hell, we could write my name in infamy if I'd taken the job. No, I took my character instead and continued doing my job, bridging the gap between our first labor pains and our lasting educational change. When I died to myself, I learned the true nonnegotiable: No matter if we win or lose, it's *how* we play the game that matters. *How* we play makes us winners. *How* we lead makes us leaders. *How* we handle what comes our way makes the difference, for the difference between a back pat and a backstab is that one severs *our* spine.

We play the game by *being tough on process and easy on people.* We're all brothers, sisters, daughters, sons, friends, neighbors, somehow related to each other, so we play the game respectfully, with the greater good in mind. Play hard, but don't play to win: Play to be a winner, someone with respect.

Suture

In the aftermath of Sean's resignation, I never fully sutured the situation in Aiken. I rightly rejected the superintendent's position; however, we had delivered a thriving baby that I felt I had best put up for adoption. My time had come, and although I fought hard to deliver change after we delivered it, I had to let go and trust God with the rest.

Moses' mother shipped him downriver because holding on would have ensured his death. Another Moses came along and rescued George Washington Carver from death after kidnappers tore him away from his mother. Unfortunately, everything that comes our way is not for us—we don't get to keep it—and it's incumbent upon us to know when to duck, when to stay, and when to let go.

I would be lying if I said my pride didn't take a hit. I felt it. I didn't want to leave. I had friends, accomplishments, and emotional ties in Aiken. I had weathered my life's most difficult storms there, but I had another lesson coming. I had to learn to catch a line drive. I took my broken-in glove, stitched the torn pieces, and ran to center field. Then, the batter hit one right between my eyes.

> ➤ I'd had a job.
>   o I'd built a career.
>   ▪ Now, I had an assignment.

Shawn Foster

Assignment

"How many square miles?" I whispered to myself. "Rhode Island inhabits 1,034 square miles, and Orangeburg County School district comprises over 1,100. I'm considering a school district that's larger than a state. Okay. I'll need leaders and leadership. Let's get started."

In 2020, I got the opportunity to serve as the superintendent of schools for Orangeburg County School District in Orangeburg, South Carolina. Less than twelve months after Sean's resignation, I departed from Aiken and took the assignment in Orangeburg. But we had problems. We had three districts; we only needed one. We hemorrhaged money; we needed some. We had a $12 million budget deficit; we needed investment funds. We had insurmountable logistical issues. We had over 1,100 square miles for potential improvement. We had an opportunity, and I had an assignment.

Before my cancer, I had a career. I thought I understood my assignment. I thought that since I worked in education and knew my purpose, *to impact the lives of children, communities, and people, and to help them become the best they can be,* I understood my assignment. That's a logical fallacy, a non sequitur. My reasoning didn't follow logic. Knowing didn't equal understanding.

We do jobs to get by, we have careers to do something, and we have assignments we are sent to do. I work in education; that's my job. I'm a superintendent of schools; that's my career—overseeing schools. I am a leader; leadership is my assignment. Someone can take away the other two, my job in education and my career as a superintendent, but unless they remove me or everybody else from my proximity, they cannot take away my leadership. I didn't create it, but I was sent to do it.

Understanding that distinction enabled me to enact change in Orangeburg. We didn't need another superintendent; we needed leadership. I thought Aiken was a tough delivery; this baby weighed thirteen pounds. I had to plan, and planning required research.

Research required boots on the ground, so when I drove to Orangeburg and had my first community meeting, I stirred up activists. I said, "There were already tons of problems before I got here. I didn't bring them down with me in my truck." I let it sink in. "I didn't bring any solutions in my truck either. We'll find the solutions here, in the people of this community." That got us started, infusing the community with belonging and initiating a firestorm of research.

The people investigating problems dug up things. The true leaders sought solutions and gathered evidence. They also revealed themselves as leaders—not by title but by action. My statement did something else: It separated the sheep from the goats. The goats blamed me for preexisting problems.

Assuming a $12 million deficit indicated frivolous spending would have been another logical fallacy, a hasty generalization—I didn't have enough evidence. Deficits have multiple origins. Consider a couple boasting a strong financial portfolio and then suffering a divorce. One partner gets nothing, while the other claims it all. Throw child support, alimony, a new living situation, childcare expenses, etc., on top of the newly penniless partner and watch the ship sink. This poor loser may have pinched pennies for years but got the short end of the stick.

We did research. Accounting and consolidation errors. Recouping funds required further investigation. Without a demographic study, we couldn't understand our options. As one could expect, with that sprawling land mass, we had schools smattered across the countryside. Strategically located facilities that were networked together would greatly reduce overall operational costs. Translation: We had to close some schools.

Considering when the individual schools were built, their disparate locations were not illogical. But times had changed. Originally, each school facilitated a need in a specific community. As the areas changed, more needs arose, so they built more schools. When I came along thirty years later, I had a bird's-eye view, so I could see we must close, consolidate, and condense.

Picture a disorganized kitchen. Typically, we put pots and pans in one area, blenders, mixers, and grinders in another, utensils in another, etc. Everything's located in the kitchen, but we consolidate items for efficiency's sake, which requires minimal mobility. Well, my kitchen looked like Momma had an episode and put rolling pins in the oven and paper towels in the fridge. At some historical point, her decisions made sense, but when I walked in, I saw calamity. And we all know what happens when somebody moves Momma's stuff in the kitchen.

I knew what would happen. The study concluded we must close nine schools. Nine. Most superintendents don't survive closing one. I asked myself, "Is it about the job, the career, or the assignment?"

I continued my research. I established over 150 town hall meetings, touched every community, made presentations and got feedback, and continued researching. Before one presentation, I knew my first rendition was not my final version, but it stimulated conversation. That provoked gathering evidence. Then, we could make well-informed decisions. *Sometimes, making a proposition draws out more truth than asking questions.* Think of Solomon, the baby, and the sword.

As I suspected, when I mentioned moving Momma's rolling pins, I got attacked. Logical fallacy number three: *ad hominem* attack. As one can imagine, I experienced nothing new here. Some accused me of planning to leave, having a girlfriend, and stealing money, and, of course, they threatened my job.

I assured everyone that I sought discovery in our initial meetings, that I'd make a recommendation during my second go-round, and that I'd decide by the third time. That brings us to two crucial elements simultaneously: My actions required large investments of communication and time.

Circling back to our 3-Step Communication Process, I followed it accordingly. I told them the plan, updated them on the progress, and told them when I'd be done. I did all this telling *before* we did anything. We'd completed studies, held meetings, and gathered research, but we hadn't made any moves yet. Leadership requires us to frontload communication. Preparing people for change may trump making a change. If people aren't prepared, the change falls apart. So, we over-communicated, which took time.

Traveling throughout the district, presenting at town hall meetings, meeting teachers, students, and staff at all the facilities, and inspecting proposals, sites, reports, etc., required large quantities of time. To prioritize my time, I divided my tasks into quadrants.

1. Important and urgent
2. Important and non-urgent
3. Urgent and unimportant
4. Non-urgent and unimportant

Explaining each quadrant's functionality proves non-urgent and unimportant at this juncture, so I'll point directly to the heart. I had to make daily, hourly, and sometimes minute-by-minute prioritizations during this season. I had a newly heightened relationship with God—especially heightened after my cancer. I also had my relationship with Tanya, our kids, and my assignment. If I only had a job, prioritization would go one, two, three, four. But, since I had an assignment, priorities intertwined. I'm a leader everywhere: It's part of me. So, I had to know *when*. I prioritized my schedule and trusted God for the outcomes.

The situation got worse. I announced the baby. People gathered at a particularly contentious board meeting, hoping to watch me squirm. We had standing room only. Some wore matching T-shirts, opposing my plan. That's logical fallacy number four: bandwagon. I sat, and I gave them the floor.

Time Out

Previously, I mentioned dividing the sheep and goats. In time, the wolves emerged, too. The goats blamed me. The wolves attacked me.

Time In

My opponents eviscerated my character. They claimed I lied, cheated, communicated behind their backs, and neglected to inform them of deficits, pitfalls, and deficiencies, generally absolving themselves of all guilt while laying it on me. They said I wanted to close nine schools under their noses. They said I wanted to destroy communities and hid it all from them. They accused me of *under*-communicating. That's logical fallacy number five: a red herring. They diverted the attention away from the preexisting budget shortfall, making the meeting about my lack of communication.

I'd had enough. I wrote the book on over-communicating. After their attack, I asked for permission to speak. They agreed, and I took my turn.

> I've been reflecting. I've made an error in judgment here, and I believe when a leader makes an error, he must own up to it. I should own up to mine. The biggest mistake I've made here is being quiet for far too long. I wanted to maintain civility. I didn't want to assassinate anybody's character. The time for that has passed. Here are the facts.

I placed three reams of paper on the table. "These are the facts." I reviewed the evidence. For every time an individual had claimed ignorance, I read the meeting minutes that proved their knowledge. They *had* attended. They *had* been informed. I also read emails that proved my opponents false. They *had* lied.

I painstakingly pushed the responsibility into the rightful owners' hands and let them hold it. I assigned blame where it belonged. After a few minutes, holding three reams of truth before a crowded room got pretty heavy, and some people's faces turned red. I didn't care. It needed to happen. I had died to my career and been reborn to my assignment. Someone had to pull the trigger.

Assigning Blame

On the evening of February 8, 1968, thirty-one protestors at South Carolina State University in Orangeburg suffered violence: Three died, and twenty-eight were injured. The violence marked a dire tragedy in U.S. history and was called the Orangeburg Massacre.[15] Orangeburg has a bleeding history.

During tragedies, people often clamor for a root-cause analysis before remedying the tragedy. They assign blame. That approach stokes the fire, politicizes the event, polarizes the community, and largely solves nothing related to the current issue: The community is swimming in crisis.

How many conclusions did you make from the opening paragraph? What internal questions did you ask? Did any of these make the list?

- Was it a civil rights protest?
- Was it race-related?
- Did it involve gun violence?
- Were law enforcement officers involved?
- Were any protestors violent?
- Did any victims get arrested?
- Did the perpetrators get acquitted?

Those are excellent questions, and they all deserve answers, but they are the wrong questions to ask during a crisis. Did you ask, "How did they communicate, console, and reestablish order?" What other questions didn't you ask that are much more concerned with people and much less concerned with politics? During a crisis, we must solve the immediate problems first, and then we can begin a root-cause analysis. But not before. As I wrote, Orangeburg has a bleeding history.

~

At 3:40 p.m., I received a phone call from the principal at Orangeburg-Wilkinson High School, "Dr. Foster, we've had a school shooting."
"How many are injured?"
"One."
"Did we catch the suspect?"
"Not yet. We're getting everybody to safety."
"Law enforcement in pursuit?"
"Yes."
"Stay calm. You know what to do."
I called my senior staff to the conference room. As I walked there, my head of security called, and I told him I was aware and to do what we had outlined in our protocols. We convened in the conference room, and I sent a quick text to the board of education about our current crisis. I pulled the superintendent of communication next to me, but before I could say anything, I received another call.
"Dr. Foster, there's been two injuries."
"Okay, any of them fatal?"
"Not at this time. One got shot in the leg, the other in the stomach."
"Is it an active shooter?"
"We're not sure. We don't know if these are separate incidents."
"Okay. Get the kids to safety. Are we all locked down?"
"Yes, and law enforcement is sweeping the interior and exterior."
"Keep me updated."
I turned to the superintendent of communications.
"Make sure we're following the process. We need two people taking notes in case there are discrepancies. As soon as we can, we need to get communication out—"
Another phone call.
"Dr. Foster, there's a third student injured, possibly a drive-by shooting."
"God help us. Thank you. Keep me updated."
We continued gathering information, quickly assembling it, and then communicating it to the community. We followed our crisis response

plan, and I received the call that law enforcement had apprehended and removed a suspect from campus.

"Guys, we must move to the school. We need to orchestrate the reunification process."

We moved to the school while buses arrived with students—yes, arrived. Law enforcement searched every single student because weapons transport matters. There could be multiple shooters, retaliatory measures, or an attempt to hide evidence. Since some students attended off-campus athletic practices, we returned them to the central hub, where they could be searched and then released to their parents.

Emergency personnel transported the victims to the hospital. We met with the sheriff's department on campus and set up our site. As they continued searching students, we assigned senior staff to specific areas. They followed suit. Our technology center served as the reunification site, so we stayed close to it and followed our protocols, designating locations for reunification, media, communication, and emergency personnel.

After communicating with the parents of both the victims and the suspect, we released further communication that we'd apprehended the suspect and that all victims had been transferred to the hospital. We hoped to squelch some insecurities; however, until parents see their children unharmed, all sorts of scenarios radiate in their minds. Many parents missed our communications, so their emotions rumbled.

The sheriff and I convened, discussing the conversation we'd have with the parents while our staff passed out water in the scorching August sun. We met with the parents first, discussed the protocols, handed out water, and explained that the victims had been transported, the suspect apprehended, and we'd release students soon. Many parents behaved gratefully; some had derogatory comments, but we had communicated our expectations clearly.

Then we met with the media. Our chief of staff had updated our local media, but we gave it to them from the horses' mouths. But first, we said, "We're not taking any questions." A reporter rebuffed us, so we explained, "This is how it's going to be." Solve first. Discuss later. And that's how we proceeded. The sheriff gave the tactical update and the information on the victims and the shooter, and I gave the school and community update, thanking the students, teachers, staff, and community for performing excellently.

We ordered pizza for our debrief while sending students home safely with their parents. With the sheriff beside me, one of my staff members said, "Dr. Foster, Tanya picked up Alyx a few minutes ago, and—"

The sheriff looked at me wide-eyed. He was shocked that I made my own daughter get searched. I'd seen Alyx earlier, standing in line. She followed the process like everybody else because a crisis is a crisis, and erratic behavior further perpetuates the crisis.

By 8:00 p.m., all the students had been released to their parents/guardians, and we had stopped our transportation services. In less than four hours, we'd completed all student searches, reunification, and facility clearances—an unprecedented task.

I closed the school for the next two days. Our crisis response plan did not mandate that action, but I made the decision. It weighed heavily on my mind because two days plus the weekend allows students a lengthy time to brood, manufacture their narratives, suffer grief and loss, and return angry. That's time on their hands I'd rather not grant but time we needed to ensure an appropriate return. We'd only returned from summer break three days prior, and due to the COVID disruption, it had been several months since we had a regular, in-person schedule. Combine all that with a violent shooting, and students could return to calamity. We wouldn't allow that.

We communicated the school closure to the community and reaffirmed that on-site and online counselors were available for the students. I did not, however, give teachers those days off. Against my senior staff's advice, I requested all teachers meet the following morning in the auditorium. My decision ruffled everyone's feathers, and the underlying tension nearly bubbled over.

At 7:30 a.m., I stood before a crowded, hurting, angry room. "I know you are upset. I wanted you present today so I could put eyes on you and see that you're okay. You have people here to lean on. Let's talk about what happened and what we can do to make you feel safer before we resume school." The mood shifted, and the teachers united, building protocols to ensure a more seamless return.

Staff swept the school for the victims' personal items. After removing them and cleaning and repairing the crime scene, we walked the grounds with the principal and deemed the school fit for return.

On Monday morning, after continual weekend communication, our community members welcomed our students back with signs, cheers, and celebration. The law enforcement officers hugged and high-fived students as they neared the building, and all involved parties clapped the students in. Students received celebrity-like treatment for returning; the prior Wednesday, they had left a crime scene. The counselors kept their offices open, and we brought in additional counseling staff for layered support.

Several staff, teachers, and students made appropriate visits to the family members of both the victims and the suspect. All involved parties had suffered a tragedy. The victims and their families suffered injury, loss, and fear. The suspect's family suffered loss, too. Imagine the floating gossip, accusations, and hatred. They also lost their child to prison. We supported all families involved the best we could, and then we addressed the root causes.

Analysis and Explanation

In Aiken, I had experienced a school tragedy. At the time the shooting began in Orangeburg, I'd already buried over sixty students due to violence, suicide, and tragic accidents. My career had begun in a hotbed of crisis at the alternative school. As my leadership capacity grew, I touched more and more lives, and tragedy's breadth grew with my responsibility. I'd experienced many crises, and I didn't want to waste more time on failure.

I'd learned never to waste a good crisis. I wanted the building of our crisis response plans to be an unimaginable time-waster because I never wanted to use them, but I wanted to rest assured that we could.

Building our crisis response plan required that we answer several questions after we built our crisis response requirements. We knew we needed a robust communication plan, safety and search protocols, a reunification procedure, and a return to school process. After we built our requirements, we had answers to the questions:

- How do we communicate?
- How frequently?
- To whom do we funnel our communication?
- How do we respond alongside the outside agencies?
- How do we align their communication with ours?
- Where do we move the students?
- When do we reunify students and parents?
- How do we support the emotions of the students, faculty, and staff, as well as those closest to the victims and suspects?
- How do we mitigate retaliation?
- How do we reestablish ourselves as a safe and effective learning environment?

The list continued.

During the COVID shutdown, we met monthly with law enforcement and enacted our crisis response plan, drills, and the action steps outlined in our crisis response book. Yes, we created a crisis response book, and yes, we practiced monthly even though we didn't have students in our facilities.

During our crisis response training, our "Stop the Bleed" protocol included applying tourniquets. If we couldn't get to the available kits, teachers learned how to use belts instead. I remember an assistant principal complaining about this training because he had more important things to do. But on the day of the shooting, teachers saved lives by cinching limbs with their belt-made tourniquets. In the aftermath, that assistant principal noted, "Dr. Foster said, 'You never know when a crisis will strike.' I'm glad we prepared." He understood my sentiment but not my belief. The time to prepare is not after a crisis; we must prepare beforehand, hoping in our hearts it never happens.

Communicating our vision remained a top priority. Before the crisis, we made sure everyone knew what to do during one. During the crisis, we focused our efforts on keeping emotions regulated and how we'd manage our return to school process. We had the communication process in place, and we had our strategic supports in place. We communicated the need for powerful community support, especially when students returned to school.

The information that we'd experienced a drive-by shooting turned out to be false. Our law enforcement officers apprehended the suspect at the baseball field, hiding out near the dugouts. We addressed that in our announcement to the community. We also addressed it when the teachers met the following morning.

I had the teachers meet that Thursday morning because I knew everyone processes trauma differently. I didn't want them staying home all weekend fearing, stewing, feeling isolated, and being disrupted when we could gather to heal one another. The teachers needed to feel safe before the students could. If the teachers gave off nervous energy, it'd infect the students before the first bell rang.

Consider a teacher returning after a tragedy, opening the door to her classroom, and discovering a victim's coat on a chairback. What about a bloodstain on the carpet? We swept the facility and the ground to remove the affected students' belongings for the teachers' and students' benefit. We cleaned to anesthetize; we reduced inflammation so we could heal. That's not hiding, and it's not equivocation. A teacher grieving before students shows humanity. A teacher breaking down before students is a super spreader. That's not to say teachers shouldn't break down. What matters is *when*.

Meeting on Thursday morning turned out to be a wise move. Adults found an opportunity to grieve with other adults and time to prepare for students. The teachers felt responsible for building the return-to-school culture and facilitating the healing process. When we communicated that the suspect had brought the weapon to school, they responded with a clear backpack protocol.

We put that in order after the crisis. We didn't inquire during the crisis, pondering gun-control laws and the school-to-prison pipeline. Solving the crisis took priority, and root-cause analysis came after. We prepared first, acted second, and analyzed third as part of the healing process. Healing had to be a top-tier priority.

I understood that we lived in a retaliatory culture. In our poverty-stricken district, many students could access weapons. "Show me your checkbook, and I'll show you your priorities." Prioritizing healing over hate became paramount. That's why we had a vigil. That's why we had counselors available. That's why we front-loaded the community with communication. That's why I hated canceling school; I knew the opportunities it created for swelling emotions to collide, leading people to choose sides rather than heal wounds.

But it worked. How do you build trust during a crisis? By focusing on solving the problems. Our response during the crisis built trust rather than destroyed it.

I'm not at liberty to give additional information concerning the suspect. All three victims survived the incident. Everyone got hurt. Remember the adage: "Hurt people hurt people"? Well, hurt people can heal people too. And healed people can take their past pain and use it to help others. Cancer taught me that.

Finally, imagine if you got that phone call at 3:40 p.m., and you knew your daughter could be at the school. She could be a victim. She could be hiding, hurt, or worse. How would you respond? When you answer that question, you'll know how to build your crisis response plan, and you'll trust it. That's what I did. I didn't need to assign blame. I understood I'd been assigned to Orangeburg for a reason.

Aftermath

Orangeburg has a bleeding history. We've experienced many massacres. *Something* should be done. And that *something* does not include finger-pointing, politicizing, and driving a dividing wedge between the community or other communities like it. If kids don't have food, why focus on guns? If drugs rule the streets, why focus on race? If all our blood runs red, why not respond like family?

In our families, if one child attacks another, we're still responsible for restraining, removing, and disciplining the perpetrator and protecting, aiding, and comforting the victim. At times, it's difficult to know who's the victim or the perpetrator. In the aftermath, we want to bring healing to all. Healing may include permanent separation because that's the only solution that affords safety. It's sad but true. But in our families, we never find freedom by pointing fingers.

Diverting our attention from an immediate issue to serve a political or personal purpose is also a red herring. Initially, hunters used cooked (red) herrings to train hunting dogs to follow a scent. Today, trained distractors use red herrings to assign blame. When we follow, we miss the issue at hand.

Shawn Foster

Assigned

Let's return to the contentious board meeting. After I dropped the hammer by reading the meeting minutes and outing certain individuals' phony behavior, after I left them standing there holding the weight of their lies, and after their faces reddened in shame, someone threatened my job. I responded, "I won't work so hard to keep a job that I fail to do the job," removing their idle threat.

That's a nonnegotiable for me. I won't work so hard to keep a job that I fail to do the job. I won't work so hard to keep a friend that I fail to be a friend. I learned that telling the truth outweighed any personal discomfort I felt because hiding the truth cost me my assignment. I could lead while hiding the truth, but I'd be leading the wrong way, which counteracted everything leadership meant to me.

I could lose my job, my career, and my friends, but I couldn't lose my assignment unless I turned my back on the truth. In fact, completing my assignment may be the very thing that costs me my job, career, and friends. But why work so hard to keep something that's not mine when I can be somebody who is? *Leaders do what's right despite personal loss.*

I'd love everybody to experience the rebirth I did when I lost my attachment to my job and latched on to my assignment. How could I say, "I won't work so hard to keep a job," with so much on the line? Because I realized I'd been reborn into my assignment. But it didn't stop there. I enjoyed the defining moment, the euphoria that accompanied stepping into abandoned living, but I enjoyed the free gift even more.

What's the free gift? Discovery, fascination, enlightenment, whatever you want to call it—I enjoyed the process of watching myself as a free man. I enjoyed every moment while behaving the way I always wanted to behave. We think we know ourselves, but do we know ourselves when we're unbeholden to others? Do we know who we are regardless of what others think? What's greater than discovering you have *more* character than you imagined?

Here's an example: When I took the position in Orangeburg and decided to close nine schools and ask for $190 million to do it, a close friend tried to talk me out of it.

"Shawn, what are you doing in Orangeburg?"

"You know what I'm doing. I'm closing nine schools."

"And you know they're going to fire you for that."

"That's the best news I've heard. They'll fire me if I close the nine schools, but they'll fire me if I don't close the nine schools. Either way, I'll get fired."

Understanding that quandary freed my spirit. I chose to do what my gut felt was right, without reservation. The school board, law enforcement, the government, or sickness could take my job. Hell, a drunk driver could impair me and take my job. But integrity—my character—nobody could take that. Only God. Since I'd get fired either way, I could throw myself into the work without fear. Not foolishly but fearlessly. And discovering that character in myself, the type of character that didn't decide based on outcomes but based on obedience, felt good.

Abandoning the hope for a positive result but doing the work anyway because it needed to be done and was part of my assignment inspired me more than working for a specific outcome—it set me free. That's when I discovered my character and liked what I saw. Imagine discovering you like yourself *more* when all the cards are on the table, and you've lost! That's lighting a stick of dynamite in a moral dilemma and watching it explode.

SOMETIMES, THE BATTLE IS YOURS, BUT THE RESULTS ARE NOT.

Discovering my true self, unshackled from expectations and pretense, made me experience life like a newborn baby experiences discovering her hands. Except, I didn't immediately shove my hands into my mouth! I had friends to make.

Making bold and courageous changes required more of me than selflessness. It required compassion. Just like we created a return-to-school protocol to ease tensions after the shooting, I developed a return-to-civility protocol after that board meeting.

Before the meeting, a community group consisting of elected officials, pastors, and retired educators had aligned against me, certain I'd come to eat the sheep. After the board meeting, I scheduled a follow-up meeting with the group and assured the shepherds that I was both sheep and shepherd and neither part wolf.

We huddled in my office, and I explained my intentions. "I have one question before we begin. Are you here to get information or for interrogation? If you are here for information, you must accept what I tell you, but if you are here for interrogation, our discussion will be fruitless because you will be displeased no matter what. I understand someone lied to you, and it hurts to discover you were fighting for a lie. But we're talking about schools and children, and if we don't work together, our children will reap the consequences."

From that pivotal meeting, a faith-action group was created. It met regularly to discuss education, law enforcement, and economic development, and it held vital sway over the community. As we aligned in our efforts, the community began to embrace progress.

I did not lose my job as superintendent, and we moved forward with our plan to close nine schools and consolidate others. We passed the bond referendum that raised $190 million! My experience in Aiken prepared me to hold on throughout the tumultuous times in Orangeburg, but my battle with cancer taught me to let go. When I let go of the results, I could focus on the people, those who stood near or afar.

After we passed the bond, I held a press conference. One of the reporters asked, "Dr. Foster, what do you say to the naysayers?"

Yet another red herring. In a moment of celebration, somebody invited me to dance on my opposition's graves. Why would I do that? The bond referendum had helped their children and mine. Instead of dancing on their graves, I should dance with the opposition. So I didn't take the bait.

"I say nothing other than we need to work together. I'll start an oversight committee." Guess who joined the oversight committee? Now that we're successful and cutting ribbons on new schools, guess who are my biggest supporters? And now that we're successful, people thank the oversight committee for doing what they do.

Meanwhile, some of the pastors from the faith-action group have become close friends. I told you I had friends to make! One of the members' sons now even works on the construction crews that build our new buildings. A once contentious relationship grew into iron sharpening iron. With the help of the oversight committee and the faith-action group, we accelerated the building programs, and we now have heavily attended ribbon-cutting ceremonies.

Do not be deceived. Everyone doesn't swim in the same direction. We still deal with different personalities and agendas, but now, when we scrap, it's over the same general ideas. And scrapping is necessary for friction to polish our ideas. As I said, I won't do so much to keep a friend that I can't be a friend. But I will be friendly. I'll give credit where it's due, regardless of how I feel. Usually, giving away credit makes me feel better, regardless of how I felt before I gave it away.

I may be writing the book, but I don't get all the credit. *The more I give, the more God gives me to give.* I make sure others get credit for what they do. That's part of leadership. When people aren't ready to lead, it's my responsibility to get them ready, and one way to get them ready is to congratulate them on a job well done and give them an opportunity to do it again.

Congratulations!

- ➢ We had three separate districts. Now, we have one. *Divided to united.*
- ➢ We had a $12 million deficit. Now, we have a $42 million surplus. *Negative to positive.*
- ➢ We had broken buildings. Now, we have three new ones, and we're building two more. *Old to new.*

Congratulations, Orangeburg County School District! We're doing the work! If any district had a recipe for failure, we did. We had financial, physical, and mindset differences, got struck by the pandemic, and then

Shawn Foster

had an on-site community tragedy. We should have disintegrated, but we didn't crumble. *We doubled down.* As a community, we grew stronger, pulverizing our adversity and building a collective team. Yes, congratulations are in order, not only for what we can see and count but also for what goes unseen.

Truth Be Told

The truth be told, I could have ended the book there. I could have built up to a climax and then laid out all the positive changes we've made. And that would have been appropriate. However, our true reason for celebration can't be measured in dollars and cents, quantified by degrees and certifications, or accredited by facilities and structures. All those things are symbols of what truly matters.

The American flag is a symbol. When we salute the flag or pledge our allegiance, we align ourselves with an idea behind the symbol, something beyond its cloth waving in the wind. The flag is tangible, but we're seeking an intangible.

On Wednesday mornings, a small group prays by our flagpole. We stand in unison, and we seek the Intangible. Sometimes, we share before we pray. On a particularly bright morning, Mr. Hayward Jean, the district director of student services and leader of our Wednesday Whispers, made a bold and courageous statement: "We're not building buildings. We're building people."

At first glance, that statement can seem trivial. With deeper evaluation, it tells a story of a divided people who banded together to build a brighter tomorrow. People who built despite disagreement. People who believed education builds people.

People discover who they can become through education. Not just students but people. Throw everything you know about public, private, or home-based education out the window and focus on the words. People discover who they can become through education.

Discovery is learning, and learning is getting educated. And within our four walls, we provide opportunities for all. Not just the students. All. Teachers grow. Staff grows. Principals grow. Everybody expands their knowledge and skills. We discover who we can become. We create scientists, doctors, entrepreneurs, teachers, lawyers, and even leaders. We create jobs and build careers, and we help people discover their assignments. The school buildings are the place, but the people within are the essence. *It's not about the symbol; it's about what the symbol represents.*

It's not about the people you impress; it's about the people you impact. That's it. Strip it all away. Get that weight off your shoulders. Throw it in the lake. Sell out. Go for broke. Do something. Don't worry about *their* expectations. Find a way to become who you want to be. Not who you've been told to be. Not who you've convinced yourself you are. Who you want to be. That's your assignment: Figure out who you want to be.

YOU'VE BEEN ASSIGNED.

Shawn Foster

The Good Race

Don't fall for it! Don't fall into the isolationist's trap when pondering who you want to be. I said to strip away others' expectations; I didn't instruct you to strip away others. And don't fear. I won't leave you alone to figure it out. We'll soon discuss a process for discovering who we want to be, but for now, please know that *good leaders are good followers.*

Pop had a peculiar way of responding when people greeted him. A friend would say, "How are you doing?"

Pop didn't say, "I'm well," or, "I'm doing great!" He didn't say, "If I were any better, there'd be two of me." When asked how he was doing, Pop said, "I'm running the good race."

I assume he borrowed that idiom from another author: "I have fought the good fight, I have finished the race, I have kept the faith,"[16] who followed another teacher who simply said, "Follow me."[17]

Pop went to be with the Lord on New Year's Eve 2023, but before he did, he dropped some conspicuous breadcrumbs to follow. I had plane tickets to Dallas, planning to watch the Cowboys play the Packers at AT&T Stadium.

Just days before flying out, I got a call that Pop had taken a turn for the worse and would be hospitalized. Pop had recently celebrated his 91st birthday, so he'd been knocking on death's door for a long time. I knew he'd be okay; he was invincible. I made a leadership decision, and I decided *when,* so I went to Dallas to celebrate with my friends.

Do you really think I flew to Dallas? Would it have been wrong if I had? Remember that piece about others' expectations?

Instead, I made an individual decision based on my relationship with Pop and how he'd mentored me from my football-playing youth all the way through my bout with cancer. I went to see Pop.

"How you doing, Pop?"

"I'm running the good race."

See, when discovering who we want to be, we don't have to take an ascetic quest into far-flung lands. As Pop said, "Everything you need, you already have." Instead, we can follow the leaders around us and then apply their examples to our individual context.

Pop did most of his leading with his hands and heart, and he gave me this leadership framework before he passed. He helped me understand what it meant to "run the good race."

To run the good race, you must know:

- What you're running for
- What you're running to
- What you're running against
- What you're running from
- What you're running with

What You're Running For

Pop ran to win. When the gentlemen who started Workaholics Anonymous pondered how to help workaholics recover, Pop took out their trash. Not really, that's hyperbole to demonstrate how much he worked, but Pop did take out the trash. He cleaned office spaces; he cleaned entire buildings. I remember him handing me a spray bottle and rag outside his "Scooby Doo Van" before we entered the BellSouth building. We scrubbed walls, polished floors, dragged trash to dumpsters, and did it with a smile on our faces. After we got home, he changed clothes and headed to the casino, where he was a floor manager. Pop worked to win his kids and grandkids a better future. He knew who he ran for and what he ran for. He ran for us.

What You're Running To

Shawn Foster

Pop also knew what to run to. He understood that those time-tested relationships that weathered adversities, failures, and triumphs mattered because those were the people who would catch you when you fall and help you get up when you've failed. Pop showed me that when I fell ill with cancer and when we won the football championship. Pop taught me what to run to and to whom to run. He also taught me to run toward the person I wanted to be: my vision of what I imagined myself becoming.

What You're Running Against

In his last few breaths, Pop showed me what we're running against. I held his hand, and he said, "I'm running the good race." We didn't have anyone in the room. There was nobody to race. Pop raced the clock on the wall. He raced against time, as we all do, knowing it'd eventually run out. His life showed me that we race against time and against our apathy and selfishness. We race against complacency and doubt. We race against those restraints that keep us from running with freedom.

What You're Running From

What are you running from? What keeps you from becoming who you are? Name it. Fear. Fear of what? Fear of failure? Fear of being too much? Fear of never having enough? Fear of isolation, loneliness, vulnerability? Pop taught me to identify what I ran from so I could know what to attack. I can't face an assailant that I don't know is there.

What You're Running With

Pop taught me to run with something in both hands. In one hand, we need to run with a partner who will support us, challenge us, and remind us of our purpose when we question or forget. In the other hand, we need to run with faith. We demonstrate faith while we run, showing what's important to us. This is not faith in something; this is faith expressed in action. If I say I love my family, I express that love, that faith, through my works.

Faith Works

I've made no bones about it. I'm a man of faith; I believe in God. But permit me to explain why that works. Humans have the capacity to put others before themselves. This is why we'd run in front of a car to save a baby in the street. We also have the capacity for compassion. This is why a small child can see an animal hurting and want to help it. We'll often sacrifice ourselves for our loved ones, pets, natural habitats, or something. We venerate and we self-sacrifice for what's outside ourselves. Even if it's just a belief we can't see. And since we venerate, faith pushes us so much further than we'd push ourselves.

Before you argue with me, hold on. Is there any situation you can contrive in which you would risk yourself? If so, that's an act of faith and an act of belief that something, some idea, some person, some moral code, is of greater importance than you. And it demonstrates that even if you died for it, everything would be all right because that person, thing, or belief is greater than you.

Now, I've heard the counterargument that when we venerate, we actually undervalue ourselves, but tell me, from your core, is that true? If you venerate the idea that your child's life is worth more than yours, is that undervaluing yourself and overvaluing your child? Or is that just the belief that some life, value, or object is greater than you? Even if it's solely for the propagation of the species?

We venerate. We worship. We'll do more for something outside ourselves than we will for ourselves. We'll become better versions of ourselves for something outside ourselves. We'll never discover who we want to be if we solely look within ourselves, to ourselves, or at ourselves because that never releases our highest essence. That's why we have goals, values, beliefs, and faith because we see something greater than ourselves out there.

So, I believe in God. You don't have to. But my belief in God gives me Someone to run for, Someone to run to, someone to run against, something to run from, and Someone to run with. My faith gives me Someone to follow, and we all do more when we have something to die for, and we all do less when we have nothing to live for.

Having faith does not exempt us from following the wrong thing, going the wrong way, or adopting the wrong value. But it supplies us with *more*. More of what we can't have taken, and it allows us to give up more of what we can lose.

Follow the Leader

As children, we played Simon Says and Follow the Leader. We learned that following leadership is a skill we can develop, and hopefully, we laughed a lot while we did it. Nothing has changed. Just because we're adults doesn't mean we've arrived. *Leadership is a journey without a destination.* We follow the clues, garner mentors, pattern ourselves after others, make mistakes, fail, and rise again. But all in all, we do better with examples.

Examples don't preclude us from individuality. Our individuality requires us to follow our gifts and proclivities but doesn't make us a cadre of one. Even the most radical thinkers, the savants of savants, had their people. People surround us. Without people, we have nobody to lead or follow. So when you strip away the expectations of others and build your "Who You Want to Be" profile, don't strip away the others. You're assigned to discover who you want to be in relation to others, not in isolation from others.

Progress Update

We have two chapters remaining. In the next chapter, I'll give some personal anecdotes of leadership at home and list some leaders in my life. In the final chapter, I'll help you build your leadership profile.

Followers

Followers fall into three categories: Conscious, communal, and captive. The voluntary follow consciously. They make adult decisions to follow, guided by volition. Communal followers follow the herd. Although they also follow consciously, they're often convinced by the pack's safety and the strength in numbers. If the pack falls away, these followers will not stay. The final group, the captives, constitute this chapter's subject, for they are our children.

While writing this book, I found myself gravitating to the subject of being a leader to my children. All leaders are not parents, but all leaders were once children. This message applies to all. The applications in this chapter help us better understand how to lead anybody following us by force and not choice. Even the term "forced follower" feels very tenuous, so hold on tight; this will be a wild ride! Before we proceed, we must distinguish between a captive follower and one who only believes they are.

A captive follower chooses either to follow or die. Their survival depends on it. They were born into it—or they've been adopted. Persons living in a democratic society who voluntarily work are not captives. They may feel like it, but they're not. Though a man named Harold, who works for Pick-a-Corporation, feels like a corporate hostage because his current level of livelihood depends on it, he is not a captive. Give him $10 million and watch him walk away. If he won't, add a few zeros. He'll purchase his prison. Harold lives in a market-driven economy and can leave his job anytime.

Stealing is an option, as is finding a new job or even hijacking government programs created for those who can't work. Many things will put food on the table. We have options, albeit some are tasteless.

Shawn Foster

Sorry, Harold, you cannot work volitionally and be held hostage simultaneously, even if your life depends on it. You can walk away. An infant cannot. At least, not yet.

A child follows an adult's rules until old enough to escape. She may become a communal follower, following only for the safety afforded in familial society, or she may become a conscious follower. Until the time she can choose, she's a captive. As leaders, we hope our children become conscious followers, but we must remember one key element. She never chose to be a leader's child: We chose leadership and children. She never had a choice.

Nonnegotiable(s)

Despite our children's lack of choice, we must maintain nonnegotiables. We can't allow ourselves to feel sorry for our children. The world won't. Instead, people will exploit and expect more from them, charging our choices on our children's credit cards. But we cannot allow our empathy to rule us; for our children's sake, we must protect them with our nonnegotiables.

A few years ago, before my kids could kick the car door open and walk into school, I'd ask them, "What are the four things Daddy needs you to do today?"

They often answered in unison:

1. Do what's right.
2. Work hard.
3. Be good to people.
4. Make good decisions.

The nonnegotiables gave them behavioral guidelines that kept them from too much trouble, gave us common ground, and gave me congratulatory opportunities. Without nonnegotiables, I'd basically scatter my children in the wind and hope everything came out okay.

Nonnegotiables represent a behavioral funnel, whereas operating without them opens the floodgates of subjectivity. Without them, children have no idea what to do. Behavior is an imaginary target.

Leaving the "What's appropriate behavior" decision to the child forces my parental responsibilities on them. That's wrong. Children need to learn to self-regulate, but they can't do this without a benchmark. They must be taught. And for me to teach them, I must have guidelines.

I understood that my children would get in trouble—it happens. Trouble has a way of finding us. However, if they practiced my nonnegotiables, they would get in way less trouble. For example, if I taught them to "do what's right," they would consider the difference between right and wrong. But that is insufficient to protect them against manipulation. Could I truly expect a second grader to do what's right in the face of adult manipulation? That's absurd. Did adults try to manipulate them? Of course. Since they were the children of a leader, more adults wanted to manipulate them in order to get what they wanted. When my children made poor decisions, whether by manipulation or through selfish desires, I had a common ground to anchor us to. And when they made good decisions, I had a reason to applaud.

I could have Johnnie Cochran as my child and still make my point. My children may disagree on what's *right,* how we define *hard* work, or what's *good,* but we agree that I expect them to seek what's right, to work rather than steal, and to do good over evil. As leaders, our nonnegotiables protect our children from evil while we expect and direct them to do good. Without this, we'll ruin their lives.

Protection

As leaders, we must protect our children. We don't over-sympathize with them because they didn't choose to be a leader's children, but we don't feed them to the wolves either. Wolves look for prey. And when they can't get fed the way they want, they resort to devious ways. They'll lure prey and then attack from all sides. Don't be deceived. If you're in leadership and you're a parent, then you must protect your children. To do so, you can follow the three Ps of protection: Preparation, Prevention, and Promotion.

Shawn Foster

Intellectual Protection

Front-load your children with intellectual protection. I tell my kids when I get promoted. I tell them when I get a raise. I tell them when my evaluation is forthcoming. I tell them about *me*, but I don't tell them everything. I don't tell them if the district plans staffing cuts. I tell them what's happening in the district that pertains to me because it directly affects them. This keeps them from surprise attacks. Wolves.

My kids know before the attack. I've prepared them intellectually and informationally. However, I haven't given them undue insight because I'd draw targets on their backs if I did. They need plausible deniability. They need to say, "I don't know," when someone asks them, and rest assured, someone will ask them. I protect them intellectually, coming and going. I front-load them with the information they need and keep them in the dark about the information they don't. That approach covers all three Ps. They're *prepared* to answer what they know, *prevented* from knowing what they shouldn't, and *promoted* to a position of trust.

> TRUST DOESN'T REQUIRE OUR CHILDREN TO KNOW EVERYTHING; IT REQUIRES US TO DISCERN WHAT TO TELL.

Physical Protection

Physically protect your children. All leadership positions require differing levels of physical protection. We must discern what level of protection we require. When I first became a principal, I visited another principal, Jerry, across town. His children attended the school, and on the day of my visit, his son Walker arrived late. He had a good excuse, but that wasn't the point. Because Walker arrived late, I witnessed their interaction, and I learned about physical protection.

Jerry said, "Son, put your bag up and get to class." I didn't think much of it. A few minutes later, Walker walked by carrying his bag. Jerry went ballistic. "Put your bag up in your locker! You know what to do! Get in my office!" I stood clueless for a minute but watched for

Knee Deep

clues to drop. Walker dropped his bag in his locker, carried his books, and went to his dad's office.

What is going on?

Jerry turned to me. "Every day, I search backpacks. I recommend kids for suspension, expulsion, and juvenile alternative school based on what I find."

"What's your point?"

"Everybody knows Walker is my son. If he carries a backpack, someone can slip in a prohibited item, and his high school career here is over. Maybe even his college opportunities."

Any kid can be targeted, but Jerry understood that his child would be especially targeted. He took precautions against it. He physically protected his son. Ironically, his son suffered physically while carrying his books, but it provided him with more protection. How do you think Walker felt about that?

Here's the tricky leadership question: How much should Jerry have considered Walker's feelings versus Walker's physical safety in this situation? Before you read any further, decide: What's the right thing to do? Remember that people often say one thing in innocuous situations, like when they're reading a book, and do other things in costly situations, like when their wife complains. What would prepare, prevent, and promote Walker best?

I learned two principles from this situation with Jerry. One, I was required to overprotect my children physically because of my position. Two, I didn't want my children to attend a school where I was the principal. Fortunately for Alyx and Aden, I got promoted before they got to junior high and high school. Or, unfortunately . . .

Emotional Protection

During Alyx's freshman year, she got real-world, firsthand experience with collateral damage. Somebody fired some shots at me, but the gunshots damaged her hearing. No, not literally, but as we all know, emotional weight often burdens us more than physical weight. Hence, the analogies of an albatross, a five-hundred-pound gorilla, and a cross.

In our district, we had a charter school. While charter schools receive public funds, they often don't receive property tax funds, and they rely more on state/local government funding, as well as charitable donations. They also operate via a contract between the state and the school district. This gives the charter more flexibility with curriculum and more or less funding depending on their situation. Our charter school received more than adequate funding.

The charter divided the district along wealth lines, not race lines. We had a majority African American school district; however, we also had impoverished students and affluent families. Many affluent families sent their children to the disproportionately overfunded charter school.

I didn't like it and made it clear I did not intend to renew the charter, but I would absorb the school into the district and make it a magnet, healthcare-focused school. *They* didn't like it. *They* shall remain nameless. Another contentious discussion spilled into the wrong hands.

I sat in my office working on some budgeting issues when Alyx texted me.

"The teacher is trash-talking you."

"You okay? How are you doing?"

"I'm cool."

That simple. I got the details at home.

"The teacher was going on about how you ostracized so many people and closed off advanced learning opportunities for students by shutting down the charter. She said you're against anything that doesn't directly benefit your district. Rylee raised her hand, but I told her to put it down. I didn't want the teacher to know."

Several weeks later, while conducting school visits, I entered that same classroom, and the teacher greeted me kindly. While she continued her lesson, Rylee said, "Alyx, you ain't going to say hi to your Daddy?" The teacher caught it, and her behavior changed immediately.

I'd taught my children that in situations involving me, the situations would correct themselves, or when I deemed it appropriate, I would step in. I never wanted them to step in.

That may not seem like emotional protection at first glance, but consider the alternative. If Alyx made a scene and told the teacher I was her dad the first time the teacher complained, it would have emotionally charged the situation. There could be retaliation. By practicing patience, Alyx got to practice being impervious to insult. The teacher didn't know she insulted Alyx, but my daughter knew and absorbed it. She didn't disrupt the rotten eggs, and they ended up on the teacher's face. Alyx had been prepared; she prevented an altercation, and she got promoted—to being a stronger human being.

Expectations

Previously, I wrote:

- Expectations without explanation are presumptions.
- Expectations without communication are silent wishes.
- Expectations without training are childhood dreams.

Some even say, "Expectations are planned resentments." However, communicated expectations create clarity. And clarity is kind. For the captive followers, the leaders' children, expectations cut both ways. As a double-edged sword, they cut a wide swath toward success but also create burdensome incisions.

Limitless Expectations

Consider the pastor's children who've witnessed their parents planting several churches. For those children, beginning a new organization seems perfunctory. You plan it, organize it, execute it, and *voilà*, you have a church, a steeple, and pews packed with people. To them, planting a church feels like having dinner or doing laundry: it's just what you do.

Now, consider how an accountant's child might react if asked to start a church plant. *You want me to do what? Talk to whom? Ask for money? It seems overwhelming.* It is overwhelming. But, saving 10 percent instead of giving 10 percent may be easy for the accountant's child and evil for the pastor's children.

For all the unnecessary pressures that leaders' children inherit, they also inherit natural expectations that blind them to roadblocks. They witness leadership. They have front-row experience dealing with conflict, naysayers, and rejection. They're inoculated against the opposition, vaccinated against the failure virus—if they choose to follow the leader. A person who is impervious to insult and convinced that success is their destination becomes very strong-willed. They become a Man—

—ning. Look at the Mannings. Archie Manning played professional football. Of his three sons, two played professional football, and the other came close. Let's get tighter. Archie didn't just play football; he earned a spot in the College Football Hall of Fame and played a legendary thirteen-year career in the NFL. At quarterback. What position did his two NFL sons play? Quarterback. Let's get even tighter. The numbers are rough, but the odds of a high school football player earning a spot on an NFL team are about .02 percent.

What are the odds of making it as a quarterback? Tighter. What are the odds of making it to the Hall of Fame as a quarterback? Tighter. If Eli gets elected to the Hall of Fame, what are the odds of having two of your three sons named to the NFL Hall of Fame as quarterbacks? And it looks like his grandson, Arch, could be on his way, too.

Obviously, I cherry-picked that example, but to the Mannings, playing NFL football seemed like a Sunday drive. They watched their dad play football like we've watched dads rake leaves. It's what he *did*. Sure, genetics, connections, and finances all played a part, but many rich, connected, and athletic people only sniff the football field from private luxury suites. Don't believe me? Check your local country club.

So, yes, being a leader's child has many downsides, but being exposed to leadership early cuts away much of the fear with one broad stroke. It normalizes high achievement. Just ask former President George W. Bush and his brother Jeb, or ask Steph and Seth Curry.

Limiting Expectations

A leader's child often doesn't see limits where others do. Their parent's behavior is normalized, being out front, taking charge, and impacting others. Maturing in close proximity to those behaviors sharpens the child's sword. Well, one side of it. But the other side cuts just as deeply.

Outsiders and insiders alike attempt to balance the equation by focusing on the leader's child's advantages and not the child as an individual. We're all familiar with the overused "My dad casts a big shadow" archetype. That's because the children of the shadows had everyone around them focusing on their advantages.

For the following example, let's use Bronny and LeBron James as handles. LeBron is the all-time NBA leading scorer, and Bronny is his son. Before Bronny's birth, people wondered if he'd be athletic like his dad. The expectations were set. People expected him to be a great basketball player, and if he turned out to be a classical pianist, then many would view him as a failure. That's an associative bias, which we do naturally as humans. We expect big to beget bigger, good to beget better, and wise to beget wiser. However, it doesn't work that way.

So, Bronny's life is laced with expectations. People believe he'll be the benefactor of millions, receive ludicrous nepotism, have the inside track on the NBA's affairs, and gain access via his father. No matter what he does, he'll walk in LeBron's shadow. People can't measure Bronny for Bronny; they measure him in relation to his dad.

Now, let me bring it closer to home. Alyx's teachers expected her to achieve at a high level, which she did. She competed for valedictorian, finished high school with a 4.6 GPA, and graduated with two associate degrees. (We had a fast-track program that allowed students to earn two associates if they took summer classes.) Of course, Alyx took those classes—meanwhile, she played competitive volleyball and received many scholarship offers for athletics. Sounds pretty impressive, right? Of course, it does.

Of course, Alyx took advanced placement classes, competed for valedictorian, and earned two degrees in high school while playing both club and school volleyball: Her daddy's the superintendent. We expect it, and we ignore the individual. We, as parents, do, and *they*, as outsiders, do. And, *of course*, there's more . . .

Without conflict, life is boring. Since Alyx earned more credits than any other graduating senior, she represented the sole graduate with two associate degrees and her high school diploma. Fortunately, in her cohort, we had two other students who finished their associate degree in December and could graduate early. We informed them they only needed three additional classes to add the second associate degree, and they jumped on it. Those two high achievers saved Alyx from experiencing a skepticism-laced graduation ceremony, "Of course, *his daughter is the only one to graduate with two degrees.*"

In three seconds, Captain Cynic could have undermined my daughter's years of hard work, dedication, and discipline with an off-handed criticism. He'd have capped her achievement with a glass ceiling. Why? Because when a leader's children succeed, we want to set the balance back to even. Then, when it serves us, we jump on the other side and make the seesaw throw the child.

More times than I can count, adults asked Alyx for the inside scoop or bludgeoned her to get more resources. I've pulled many adults aside and explained, "Alyx is a child. She's a student. You may think she has access to those things, but she doesn't, and to put her in a position to leverage her relationship with me to *your* advantage is wrong." They couldn't *see* her because they already *saw* me.

Alyx's celebratory achievements are limited, and her ability to experience school as a typical student is also limited. She walks in my shadow whether she wants to or not. And as I wrote, this is not limited to any specific arena. I'm in education; LeBron's in the NBA. So, how are we to then live? Do we stop shining our light because it casts a long shadow? Do we withhold our God-given abilities from the world because it *shall* negatively impact our children? Do you hope this isn't a rhetorical question?

Balance

I've told you from the beginning that I'll use aphorisms, maxims, epigraphs, proverbs, and parables, so it's time for a proverb. "A false balance is abomination to the LORD, but a just weight is his delight."[18] We often instinctively want to balance nepotism to favor ourselves. If we suspect nepotism—say Bronny James playing NBA basketball—then we'll root for Mac McClung to take his place because it's so unfair. Although McClung playing NBA ball doesn't do anything for us, it balances the equation in our minds, so at least we *feel* better—like there's some type of justice. We don't feel so powerless. But, an hour later, if we bumped into Bronny in the parking lot, we'd use him to get our picture with LeBron or at least score something for our kids or grandkids.

That doesn't create balance for Bronny or us. We're using reverse nepotism to balance nepotism. And often, leaders overwhelm their children with unreasonably high expectations to eliminate the appearance of nepotism. We don't want others to feel; we don't want our kids to feel; we don't want anyone to feel, so we try to control everyone's feelings. That's not balance. That's control.

To create balance, we must quit focusing on balance and focus on the fulcrum.

Direction

As leaders, we're responsible for directing our children. We're not responsible for equivocating, downplaying, mitigating, diluting, or minimizing our leadership abilities. We're responsible for leading. We direct the way by leading the way. Sometimes, we direct the way by being the way.

Look at a fulcrum. Pick up a scale evenly by the fulcrum, and the scale will remain balanced. Lead it where to go. Quit ladening it with false weights on each side. Adjust the fulcrum. Focus on leadership. Our children need our leadership; they don't need us meddling with the scales. We'll just create a false balance. What they need is for us to lead them in developing their identity—their self-image.

We've all seen it. A parent incidentally implies that their child is irresponsible.

> Child: "Are you saying I'm lazy?" (Defensive)
> Parent: "No, of course not. I didn't mean it that way." (Defensive)
> Child: "But I really love the dog." (Defensive)
> Parent: "Oh, I know you do." (Conciliatory – self-defense in disguise)

Or

Child: "Are you saying I'm lazy?" (Defensive)
Parent: "Yes." (Accusatory)
Child: "Dad! You never see anything good in me!" (Defensive)
Parent: "Well, start doing good things, and I'll see them." (Accusatory – self-defense in disguise)

And we can't wait to get out of that situation. Everyone's trying to balance emotions and tension. What if, instead of piling weights on both sides, we teach our children self-image through the lenses of grace and truth?

This is not a panacea; it's a suggestion. First, a few thoughts on self-image. Nobody else defines your self-image. It's yours. You don't have to defend it because it exists inside you. Nobody can take it. Someone can take your life, but they cannot take your self-image. They can challenge your perception, but they can't take it. Clearly, one could alter it through psychosis-inducing substances, but in the end, a true self-image comes from the self. So, we can direct our children to practice actions and thinking that help promote their self-image. Practices and thinking that work for them, not us. It's their self-image, remember?

We must direct our children to be gracious. Teach them, "Everyone is entitled to their opinion of me." When people say and believe evil things about our children, we can teach them to be gracious. Others are entitled to *their* thoughts. We are entitled to *our* thoughts. And their beliefs needn't change our perception of our*selves*. Why should we change our beliefs based on another's experience of us? That's their experience. Be gracious, but don't be double-minded.

Be truthful. People have negative biases, so we point out the negatives, but we can direct our kids toward the truth. The truth is we are far more valuable than our flaws. The quicker our children comprehend their value outweighs their flaws and their value outweighs others' perceptions, the more our children will learn to shine their light. And when they shine their light, it will overcome that long shadow.

They'll follow my angel's advice: *"Remember to be who you are."* Be truthful, and don't be divided.

My wife and I have a saying: "We don't let those things happening around us happen to us." That's the essence of leadership. We *influence*. We're not influenced. We must direct and expect our children to protect themselves by shining their light. That sets the captives free. When we do, they'll either consciously choose to follow us or not to follow us. Either way, they'll have broken their shackles. They'll realize all good leaders are good followers, and their light didn't come from within. It came from above.

Shawn Foster

Faith

In the beginning, I asked if leaders are born or built. I wrote *both* and *neither*. I took a long, winding road to bring us back to this question. "Are leaders born or built?" We're about to *build* our "Who I Want to Be" leadership profile, so I must believe leaders are built, right?

Right?

Look again.

Good leaders are born *again*. We're both. We're all born. We have specific characteristics. We grow. We live. We die. Our makeup defines us. And our experiences define us. For those willing to find it, we can *experience* dying to ourselves and being *reborn* to our assignment. It's both.

Without faith, it's impossible to lead. Leaders take ideas and forge into the unknown, expecting the idea to work. We don't know if it will. We can't. If we did, we'd be God because we could predict all outcomes. Then, we'd create all the outcomes. Instead, we believe the ideas will work. We have faith. We practice it. Sometimes we're right, and sometimes we're wrong. But faith matters.

Roll Call and Role Call

What do the following characters have in common?

Grandma	Coach	Dr. Alford
Mom	Coach Abrams	Tanya
Pop	Coach Young	Dr. McMiniman
Mr. Willie	Dr. Gilmore	Cyrus
Mr. Greg	Dr. Talley	Jamaal Dukes

Knee Deep

Alyx	Nicole Thompson	Lisa Dawson
Brian Linder	Gavin Fisher	
Dr. LaVern Byrd	Sharell McDowell	

They all had uncompromising faith. They believed their behavior had transcendent value. They did not compromise themselves or their values or hurt others to lead me. But they did die to themselves for me. Sometimes daily.

Mom didn't enjoy watching her boy get the snot knocked out of him on the football field. She didn't enjoy Coach screaming at me any more than he enjoyed doing it. She hated seeing me come home dizzy and trembling from K-Mart Distribution, just as she hated when I came home drenched from chemotherapy. But she did not compromise her faith in the transcendent value of these experiences.

Tanya too. She stood by me through chemo and cancer and through board meetings when people called her husband vile names and threatened our family's livelihood. She didn't stoop. She stood.

Mr. Willie and Mr. Greg both made sure I got home safely. They didn't compromise the other passengers, but they didn't leave me behind either. Neither did Pop. Not even in his death. He left me with the transcendent message: "Everything you need, you already have."

What about Cyrus? He had more faith than I did. He demonstrated it. He put evidence down and slid it across the table. I could hold his faith in my hand after he passed. He didn't compromise to keep my friendship. He died to his feelings and said something I needed to hear, even if it hurt me. His actions are currently transcending my experience and pocketing themselves in yours.

Time would fail me to call the rest of the roll, but you can see the role each one played as a leader. *Leaders believe their actions have transcendent value, and that's the definition of faith.* So, my list of leaders shares one common attribute: faith.

Who Do You Want to Be?

You don't need an exhaustive list to determine who you want to be. You don't need bullet points to build your leadership profile. You need one

Shawn Foster

question to answer the others, such as "What's my assignment?" or "How do I find my purpose?"

Ready? The question you must ask yourself daily is "What would I do if I died to myself and was reborn?"

Progress Update

We're done. Don't forget to ring the bell.

About the Author

Dr. Shawn Foster has lived a full life. Born into poverty and raised in the projects by a single mother, he never looked at his disadvantages; he searched for his advantages. Grateful for his foundational upbringing, Shawn excelled in sports and leadership, leading his college football team to a championship season when, a few years prior, they had not won a game. As a young man, he joined the educational ranks, met and married his beautiful wife, Tanya, and continued to climb the educational ladder.

As a first-generation college graduate, he earned three additional advanced degrees before he turned twenty-nine, and at age thirty-eight, he led a district as the deputy superintendent. Then, Stage IV cancer struck. As the father of two small children, fighting the battle of his life shaped his unique perspective on leadership. He leads from the cutting edge.

Dr. Foster serves as a distinguished educational leader with over two decades of experience in school and district transformation. As the superintendent of Orangeburg County School District (OCSD), he is committed to advancing academic excellence, equity, and innovation in K-12 education. His extensive career spans multiple leadership roles, including serving as a school counselor, assistant principal, principal, and deputy superintendent/chief officer of operations and student services.

Under his leadership, OCSD has undergone a significant transformation in instructional practices and student opportunities. He has championed strategic initiatives to improve educational outcomes, ensuring all students receive a rigorous and high-quality learning experience. Notably, he led efforts to secure a $190 million bond referendum, supplemented by an additional $40 million investment, to facilitate the construction of new schools and the modernization of educational

Shawn Foster

infrastructure. His visionary leadership and systemic reforms have positioned OCSD at the forefront of educational innovation.

A testament to his commitment to pioneering educational advancements, Orangeburg County School District has been recognized as a member of the League of Innovative Schools under Dr. Foster's leadership. This prestigious national network, composed of forward-thinking school districts, is dedicated to leveraging technology, research, and best practices to drive meaningful improvements in teaching and learning. Through this distinction, OCSD collaborates with leading educators, policymakers, and researchers to implement cutting-edge strategies that enhance student success.

Dr. Foster's influence extends beyond OCSD through his active participation in numerous professional organizations and advisory boards that shape educational policy and practice at the state and national levels. He serves on the Executive Committee of the South Carolina Superintendents' Roundtable, where he collaborates with state leaders to drive systemic improvements in public education. As a member of the South Carolina High School League (SCHSL) Executive Committee, he plays a pivotal role in shaping policies related to interscholastic athletics and extracurricular programs. Additionally, he serves on the National Institute for Excellence in Teaching (NIET) Advisory Board, contributing to national conversations on educator effectiveness and instructional leadership.

Further demonstrating his dedication to educational equity and institutional advancement, Dr. Foster is a member of the Advisory Board for MUSC Hospital Orangeburg, where he works to strengthen partnerships between education and health care to support student well-being. He is also a Riley Institute Diversity Fellow—a distinction that underscores his commitment to fostering inclusive educational environments—and a Racial Equity Leadership Network (RELN) Fellow through the Southern Education Foundation, where he engages in high-impact initiatives to address systemic disparities in education.

Dr. Foster's exemplary contributions to the field of education have earned him numerous accolades, the latest being his recognition as the 2025 3A/2A/1A Superintendent of the Year by the South Carolina Athletic Administrators Association (SCAAA). This prestigious honor reflects his unwavering support for student-athletes, commitment to athletic and extracurricular excellence, and dedication to fostering well-rounded student development.

As a devoted husband and father, Dr. Foster remains steadfast in his mission to shape the lives of students positively and to elevate the educational landscape of Orangeburg County and beyond.

Shawn Foster

Acknowledgments

Behind every great leader is another great leader. Before every great leader is another great leader. Beside every great leader is another great leader. Great leaders are bookended and guard-railed by other great leaders. These are mine.

Tanya,
We've taken a wild ride together. I've been part of your story, and you've been part of mine. I suppose it's *our* story. Thank you for your stability when I couldn't stand, for picking me up when I could only fall, and for standing with me despite it all. You are a bright light on a dark day, a calm touch in a chaotic storm, and a string of laughter when we both need it most. I'm grateful to have spent these twenty years with you, and I look forward to many, many more. I respect and admire you, and you know it, but I will tell you again: I love you, you're my better half, and walking hand-in-hand with you is the best choice I ever made. I never would have thought I could have you as my wife, even in my wildest dreams!

Mom,
From my first memories, you've led me with compassion and love. You taught me that love has no boundaries: Geography, time, and not even death can stop it. Love continues through it all. Thank you for giving your life for me, for showing me you love me with your hands, heart, and hope. I wonder now if the key you tied around my neck was a symbol of your love—the key to your heart. You taught me to lead when all I could do was follow.

Grandma Foster,
You were my grandma, and like a second mother, all rolled into one. Thank you for teaching me that true leaders care despite the circumstances. Your life demonstrated that more and less fortunate were only titles and that we were all fortunate enough to give something. In your home, I received instruction in character, compassion, and loyalty.

Knee Deep

The bond your children and grandchildren share testifies to the principle you taught: Family sticks together through thick and thin. Although you've moved on, I've been making these candied yams without you, but I know you've been watching over me.

Grandma Walker,
Because you are the backbone of the family, I've expected you to always be there. For Pop, for Dad, for the rest of the family, and especially for me, you've been our pillar. I've always wondered how the quietest woman in the room could be the loudest and how the least mobile could get the most done! I bet you still don't have your driver's license, do you? Your quiet confidence taught me that a person who respects themself commands respect. Thank you for teaching me to find a way when there was no way.

Pop,
It has not been the same without you. Sometimes, I'll stare through the window and watch the leaves blow in the breeze, or I'll see the grass ruffle in the wind, and I'll think of you. I can't see the breeze, but I know there's a mighty force behind its quiet movement. You taught me that. You showed me that the will in a man can't be measured by his exterior, and the faith of a man shows through the work of his hands. Whenever I wonder if I have enough, I look at the effects of a gentle breeze and know that though I can't see it, I already have everything I'll ever need.

Monica, Terri, Cheryl, Regina, and Lynn,
Ya'll didn't think you would get an individual acknowledgment, did you? I hope not because you taught me the power of the collective and that it really does take a village. I've often said I'm fortunate that such strong women raised me. You're all strong individuals and an even stronger team. Thank you for teaching me that leaders have individual gifts, talents, and abilities, but the good ones work together in shared responsibility for others. I've never walked alone because I have known you were all rooting for me all along.

Shawn Foster

Alyx,
I've been inspired by your ability and your passion to do well. You are my daughter, and I've appreciated watching you grow. Your thoughtfulness is astounding, even dumbfounding at times. In your eyes, I see your passion for people, and in your actions, I see how compassionate you are. People's feelings matter to you because you can see their emotions inside—and that's good. Continue to use that, and know that Daddy loves you, and I'll always be here watching you grow.

Aden,
You're precocious; you know that. You're a hard worker; keep it up. What I appreciate most about you is that you are calm under pressure and cool under fire. Squabbles don't ruffle your feathers, and tensions don't knock you off track. I love seeing those characteristics shining through because I know it means you will be all right. Even so, know I love you, and I'll always be here watching you grow.

Quick Tips, Quips & Trips

Quick Tips

- Be tough on process and easy on people.
- Prepare for the storm.
- Never waste a good crisis.
- Deciding to follow the leader is a leadership decision.
- Authority is bestowed, not taken.
- We must give people a taste of leadership to see if they're hungry.
- Leaders look for other leaders to help when they can't.
- Character doesn't allow others' actions to disrupt it.
- Leaders finish before they leave.
- We develop discernment when we experiment.
- We must face our fears to experiment.
- Faith will take us further than our fears.
- The price we pay today may be the investment of a lifetime.
- Children and adults are different: Treat them that way.
- A failure who gets up will eventually beat a winner who gets down.
- Motivate the uninspired. Train the unknowing.
- Lead the way for those who don't know the way.
- Befriend leaders and follow their lead.
- Expectations without explanation are presumptions.
- Expectations without communication are silent wishes.
- Expectations without training are childhood dreams.
- As leaders, we must align people with experimental hardships.
- As leaders, we must seek solutions.
- As leaders, we must know when to quit or continue.
- When preparation isn't enough, sometimes we provide.
- You can't make a horse drink, but you can lead them to water.
- You need the right people; look for them.
- Leaders test character.
- Leaders offend to see if followers take it or overcome it.

Shawn Foster

- ➢ Leaders seek solutions, not validations.
- ➢ Suspicions are not evidence.
- ➢ Good people behaving badly is still bad.
- ➢ Character decisions are easy when we're unbeholden to others.

Quick Quips

Good leaders provide top-notch communication.
Showing up without an answer beats skipping out with one.
You have to show up.
I don't think your dad's going to beat this cancer thing.
The best leadership decisions often come from those who commit to following the leader.
How do we know when to believe what and what to believe when?
Giving people what they want from you doesn't always
change their behavior toward you.
Some battles are not yours to fight.
Leaders value character over self-justification.
We don't need a lot of people; we just need the right people.
We don't quit when we are tired; we quit when we are finished.
Leaders, we must ensure followers know and know how.
Leaders do what's hard, even when it breaks their hearts.
Leaders create leadership opportunities, so followers have someone to follow.
Remember what I wrote about plans?
Good leaders don't give up 50 percent of $1 million to get 100 percent of $10.
Sometimes, the battle is yours, but the results are not.
You've been assigned.
Trust doesn't require them to know everything; it requires us to discern what to tell.

Quick Trips

3-Step Communication Process

1. Tell people what you're going to do.
2. Update them on the progress.
3. Tell them when you're done.

3-Step Service Builder

1. Dig the hole. (Say yes!)
2. Plant the tree. (Build service habits/practices.)
3. Nurture the roots. (Invite others to serve with you.)

Running the Good Race

1. What You're Running For
2. What You're Running To
3. What You're Running Against
4. What You're Running From
5. What You're Running With

Leading Our Children

1. Protect (Prepare, Prevent, Promote)
    a. Intellectual
    b. Physical
    c. Emotional
2. Expect
3. Direct

Shawn Foster

Notes

[1] Anna Robertson Brown Lindsay, *What Is Worth While?* (New York: Thomas Y. Crowell & Co., 1893), 12, https://archive.org/stream/whatisworthwhile0000unse/whatisworthwhile0000unse_djvu.txt.
[2] Matthew 7:24–25.
[3] Jim Elliot, *The Journals of Jim Elliot* (Grand Rapids: Revell, 1978), 108.
[4] *Global Leadership Forecast 2025*, Development Dimensions International (Pittsburgh: DDI, 2025), 5, https://media.ddiworld.com/research/global-leadership-forecast-2025-report.pdf.
[5] Luke 8:18.
[6] Luke 12:2.
[7] *Merriam-Webster's Dictionary*, "opportunistic," accessed January 13, 2025, https://www.merriam-webster.com/dictionary/opportunistic.
[8] *The Last Dance*, directed by Jason Hehir, ESPN Films and Netflix, 2020.
[9] Dale Carnegie, *How to Win Friends and Influence People* (New York: Simon & Schuster, 1936), 8.
[10] Proverbs 16:18.
[11] Proverbs 19:21.
[12] Hebrews 11:1 (KJV).
[13] Proverbs 14:30 (NIV).
[14] See Malcom Gladwell's *Tipping Point: How Little Things Can Make a Big Difference*, and *Revenge of the Tipping Point: Overstories, Superspreaders, and the Rise of Social Engineering*.
[15] "Orangeburg Massacre," History.com, last modified August 5, 2021, https://www.history.com/topics/1960s/orangeburg-massacre.
[16] 2 Timothy 4:7.
[17] John 1:43.
[18] Proverbs 11:1.